THE ENERGY TO LEAD

PRODUCT

LEADERSHIP

PROCESS

PEOPLE

THE THERMODYNAMICS
OF LEADERSHIP

TERRY J. WOYCHOWSKI

ISBN: 978-0-692-22117-4

First Edition, June 2014
10 9 8 7 6 5 4

Book design by Norm Williams, nwa-inc.com

Printed in the United States of America

DEDICATION

Authors Post Script: (January, 2014)

Several years have passed since I first jotted down the notes that made up the content of this book and getting it into the hands of a publisher. Much has changed and since then I was given the opportunity to work in global assignments as a VP for General Motors that helped open my eyes to many cultural elements of leadership. I have also had the opportunity to continue to work with several small groups of aspiring leaders that go by team names such as "ARMY", "College", "Knights" and most recently, "Apollo". It has been my privilege to help teach and mentor these groups and to glean new insights into leadership with every conversation we have. I smile each time one of them demonstrates great leadership on their own as they grow and prosper in their careers and in their lives.

I have also taken on a new position with a global automotive tier one supply company named AAM where I have the opportunity to serve as the Senior Vice President of Engineering and Quality. AAM is a fantastic company that engineers, manufactures and sells automotive driveline and metal formed products. This too is a target rich environment for learning more about leadership, which I get to be part of on a daily basis. I'm pretty sure there will be another book in here someday.

Perhaps my biggest promotion since I finished this book was the day that I got promoted to Grandfather. My son Justin, mentioned in these pages has not only gotten married to his sweetheart Elle a few years back, but they have recently presented us with the most wonderful treasure in a granddaughter named Ember. If I would have known how wonderful it feels to be a grandfather or "The Chief" as I am being affectionately called, I would have had more children myself. My middle daughter Jamie has recently married a wonderful man named Blayne, and they have started their new lives together while my youngest, Jenna is attending college in Michigan. I will not mention the University by name, but "Go Green!" echoes through our house regularly. I am thrilled as I watch my children grow and strive to be men and women of faith, of character, of strength, of honor and of leadership. They are a father's pride.

With this in mind I would like to add to my list of gratitude and acknowledgment a great thank you to Elle for taking on the task of getting this book published. For years she saw this on my "To Do List", and being an astute student of leadership herself, took on the task of getting this from a file in my computer to a written form we could call a book. Thank you Elle, for making this life event possible for me. Without you, there would be no first edition. (By the way, any typos or errors one my find in this book, be advised that it is not Elle's fault. I had so many of them, and army of editors could never find them all. Some I even put in there on purpose to see if the reader was paying attention enough to catch them... Remember, I am an engineer.)

I really want to add a dedication of this book to my granddaughter Miss Ember. Holding her in my arms, rocking her as we read a story book or dancing her to sleep on my shoulder is a life treasure that I would not trade for anything. I truly want to dedicate this book to her, and to any and all of my grandchildren to follow, (may there be many). It is to them that I will strive to become a better leader, so that I might help make this a better world that they will soon inherit. It is to them that my prayers will be extended that they will grow to be men and women of honor, of valor, of courage and of unquestionable character. May they each learn and grow to become great leaders in their own right, and to continue to make this a better world from the day that they are born.

Stay Strong,
Terry J. Woychowski

TABLE OF CONTENTS

FOREWORD

By Wes Dupin,
Daybreak Community Church – Hudsonville, MI

It's funny how an off-hand comment, spoken at the just the right moment can end up crystallizing a lifetime's worth of learning. That's what happened to me.

I am the founder and lead pastor of Daybreak, a church near Grand Rapids, Michigan. Back then my son, Clint, served as youth pastor for our church. His off-hand comment was, "Dad, you need to meet the father of one of my college interns. I think you'd really hit it off." Honestly, the comment did not grab my full attention until he told me that the intern's father was the chief engineer of General Motors. That's the day that Terry Woychowski came into my life.

As with a lot of my friends, Terry and I first connected through church. Terry is a few years younger than I am and earned his success through leading the huge automobile corporation through a great and turbulent time. I found him to have a lot of wisdom in the area of leadership. So as time passed and our friendship grew, I found him to be a great leader and a natural born mentor.

I watched Terry hand pick several young men and woman at General Motors who he believed to have a lot of potential for growth and leadership. He invited them into his life and met with them each week. Terry would be totally open and transparent with them, telling them everything about his successes and his failures. This included his personal life, his business life, and his relationships. All of it. He would share the books he'd read with them. He would quote the Bible often, sharing the chapters and verses that had helped him in his walk with Jesus Christ.

Time has marched forward, and Terry has "graduated" many of these young men and women. Many of these "graduates" are now leaders at General Motors and other similar, top notch companies. Many of these young leaders are also mentoring others to become future leaders. Paying it forward as it was shared with them.

Terry has been my mentor for more than ten years. He has sparked a question that I ask myself every day of my life. That question is, "How can I become a better leader?" He has challenged me many times to constantly search for new things to learn and ways to grow. We both love the outdoors, especially if "adventure" is involved. For the last several years, I have selected my own group of men to invest in as leaders. And, I always invite Terry to join our team. Not only because he is a great friend, but also to teach all of us what it looks like to be a great leader.

Most of our leadership adventures include a pair of hiking boots, fifty-pound backpacks, and awful tasting freeze-dried trail food. A few of our trips have included hiking the Grand Canyon (rim to rim), Yosemite National Park, Isle Royale (forty miles), the Tetons (where we encountered a grizzly bear), Maroon Bells in Aspen Colorado, and many others. I remember one time while hiking in the Maroon Bells we had climbed much of the day at an elevation above 10,000 to 12,000 feet. We were tired and exhausted.

We finally stopped for a break, laid our backpacks down and stared over at the next mountain pass we had yet to climb. But Terry remained on his feet and started quoting word for word a passage on commitment and perseverance from a great leader of the past. It probably was a page out of the life of Abraham Lincoln or Teddy Roosevelt. I'm convinced he has read every book ever written on the life of Teddy Roosevelt. Regardless of who he quoted, I know that each of us got back on our feet and hiked to the next mountain pass. The short "speech" worked. He is truly an inspiration.

Terry has also taught me "success is not achieved by leadership alone." He had made it very clear that a good leader makes sure they are surrounded by the right people, that there are always open lines of communication in all matters, and that there is a strong commitment by all. Simply put, Terry's voice should be heard by all those who aspire to lead thoughtfully and effectively in their own lives.

I believe the lessons and insights in this book are more given to raising difficult questions than offering simple answers or solutions. This great leader reminds us that true leadership is a demanding vocation that requires would-be leaders to summon that which is best and strongest within themselves and act upon it. He will challenge you to focus your mind on the agonies of leadership, the "hurtin' decisions" that have kept a Teddy Roosevelt, a Margaret Thatcher, a General Motors CEO, or the pastor of a growing church awake at 4 o'clock in the morning.

I've been leaning on Terry Woychowski's advice and counsel for ten years. I often find myself asking, "What would Terry do?" I am so glad you get to meet him here. I believe God has much to say to all of us through his words.

Well done, Terry

THE ENERGY TO LEAD: THE THERMODYNAMICS OF LEADERSHIP

INTRODUCTION

T he first time I presented my thoughts on the Thermodynamics of Leadership was during a graduation ceremony for masters students at Indiana Wesleyan University. I had already delivered two addresses that day to the undergraduates, and now I was looking forward to speaking in the evening to the graduate students. My wife, Shelly, along with my Pastor Dan Steinhart and his wife, Jean, had made the trip for what was also to be a special day for me. The Trustees of the University had graciously voted to confer on me an Honorary Doctorate degree for my work in the field of engineering and leadership.

Even though it was a serious occasion, I felt some levity was in order. I told the students that as an engineer I was pleased when the dinner discussion with the President and his Staff held prior to the event had turned to science. The question posed at our table was, "What do you think is the most important scientific discovery of the last one hundred years?"

One professor, I remarked, had insisted that it was the discovery of electricity. He pointed out how total and pervasive it is in our life and society. Another well known and respected professor on campus insisted that it was not electricity, but rather the harnessing of the power of the atom.

I looked intently at the audience and said, "But your President, Dr. Barnes, he is a man of deep thought. He had considered the question for several minutes then announced, `I believe that the most important scientific discovery of the last one hundred years is definitely... *the thermos bottle.'*"

"The thermos bottle?" I said to him, nearly choking on my prime rib, "Why a thermos bottle?"

"Well," he explained to me, "Think about it -- when you put hot things in it, they stay hot."

"Yes, that's true."

"And when you put cold things in it, they stay cold."

"Yes, that too is true."

He looked around the dinner table and capped off his thought with a Socratic question, *"So how does it know?"*

There was polite laughter in the audience (in deference to the President). I looked across the smiling faces of the graduates and told them, "Now you know why they asked *me* to speak to you about thermodynamics rather than your President!"

With that clearly apocryphal story aside, I began my speech, unknowingly starting to form the basis of this book. I purposely had prepared this unique address on "The Thermodynamics of Leadership" for two reasons.

Reason number one is that I felt that the graduates could not consider themselves educated at a "Masters" level unless they possessed at least a rudimentary understanding of the basic laws of thermodynamics. Thermodynamics is the study of energy, and what is life if it is not simply harnessed and directed energy and power? To understand life you must understand energy, and you can not understand energy unless you understand the fundamental laws that govern it. Ergo -- the importance of this topic.

Reason number two is my conviction that, "It's all about leadership." Once they received their diploma that evening and would hang it on their "I Love Me" wall, it would not only certify an education achievement, but it was to also serve as the Magna Carta of their personal leadership.

As graduates of this premier University, they had been prepared to impact the world for Christ, to be used by God to expand His kingdom, and to lead others in this endeavor. Knowing the commitments of the university to service based leadership, it only seemed right that the final words imparted to them should be aimed directly at this topic

The following is the meat of what I presented. It is a brief discussion of the three fundamental laws of thermodynamics and their application to leadership. The engineer or scientist looking for an in-depth dissertation on the subject of thermodynamics will be sorely disappointed. The laws are in simple and concise form for the express purpose of providing a framework for explaining their relationship to effective leadership.

Those also looking for the final word on leadership will also be left wanting. Leadership is a very big topic and a lifetime can be devoted to its study. I share what are the lessons and insights I have learned over nearly three decades of intense and rewarding involvement in the corporate world and the church. Hopefully, what is presented here will convince you, as I am convinced, *"It's all about leadership."*

ACKNOWLEDGMENTS

I recently received an unexpected and deeply moving recognition from my Alma Mater, Michigan Technological University. In the spring of 2007 they inducted me into their "Academy of Mechanical Engineering and Engineering Mechanics". I had often walked past the portraits of the men and women who made up this academy and whose images graced the lobby of the ME-EM building at M.T.U. and had secretly wondered what a person needed to do and accomplish in order to be recognized and elected into this special group. Strolling the campus many years post graduation allowed me to reflect on the many challenges and struggles that I had endured during my career and life that had brought me to the point of being considered for this prestigious award.

Following the presentation of the award at the induction dinner party, I was given the opportunity to say a few words of acknowledgement and appreciation. As I sat to compose the acknowledgement for this book, many of the same words come to mind and seem most appropriate.

First off I acknowledged my mother Margret. As I thought back on my education at M.T.U. she was the one who always had faith in me, and continually expressed her confidence that I was up to whatever challenge might come my way. Of all the character traits that a leader needs, confidence needs to be ranked highly. When ever I had doubts about myself, I know my mother never shared them.

Secondly I acknowledged my children. Not only have they provided me with a wealth of experience and acted as my personal proving ground of family leadership training, they have allowed me to use our life experiences together in my talks and writings. I know they sometimes feel like the cannon fodder for my illustrations and jokes, but they always play along as willing partners with me. Most importantly, they have always been good children, in thoughts and in deeds. Their character and behavior made parenting easy, and allowed me to dedicate my discressionary efforts on projects and activities that helped me become a more influential leader. I owe Justin, Jamie and Jenna many thanks.

Lastly, and most importantly, I told the President of the University, and the presiding ME-EM Chair, that if I were only allowed to share one bit of advise to the graduating students that had been invited to join us, of all the advise I could give them, (and this book contains many pages of just such advise), I would distill it all down to this, "Marry well!" I can not express enough how important of a point this has been in my life. My wife Shelly has been my partner and complement in every element of my life since we took the vows to do so on a warm summer day in August in 1980. No person can achieve anything of true and lasting significance, or become a vital part of any grand effort much larger than themselves, unless they are totally supported and enabled to do so. Over the years it would be much easier to count the number of dinners I have made it home on time to than it would be to count the opposite. As many comments or looks of disappointment or disapproval that might be expected, none came. Only the warm welcome home from yet another tough battle, and the comfort and support of the one here on earth who loves me best. Without her, I could do nothing and I would be nothing.

As I have put the finishing touches on this book, a few of the leaders who have had the greatest impact on me, and have invested in my leadership training have come to mind. At the great risk of omitting some, of which I will apologize in advance, permit me to name a few.

The team of Chiefs who co-labored so seamlessly and united with me in the creation of our Full Size Trucks, Tim Herrick, Mark Cieslak, Jully Burau, and Jeff Luke. These are some of the finest leaders I have ever worked with. If I have done anything right in my time at GM, it was to assemble this team and unleash them on important programs. Books could be written about their personal leadership and character.

Other great men at General Motors have influenced me over the years. Names such as Dan Mahannah, Carl Freeman, Arnie Mummert, Ken Sohocki, Ralph Tredway, Tom Davis, Tom Stephens and Guy Briggs have all left their marks on me, (some in the form of scars), all of them inspired me to become a better leader. There are many more, but seeing as how they are still at GM, discretion tells me just to acknowledge them as great men and women I respect and admire. Hopefully they know who they are.

Keeping it all together has been my Technical Assistant, Vickie Teetsel, who has gone on and become an excellent executive and leader in her own right. She is perhaps one of the best leaders I have ever worked with. She served as my Chief of Staff, personal counselor, advisor and overall sounding board. I can not imagine taking on the dragons associated with the Second Law of Thermodynamics without her aid.

Outside of GM, John Thomas has been a good friend and advisor. He is a visionary leader who leaves me inspired and motivated every time we get together to think out loud and try to solve some of the world's tough problems. Roy Link also set an example on what a strong leader, CEO, and friend should look like. I appreciate the impact both of these men had on my life.

Two spiritual leaders have played a very important role in my life, Dan Stienhart and Wes Dupin. These men are not only good leaders in their own right, they are shepherds and caretakers of my soul and my spirit. They have convinced me that I am not a human doing, but a human being and that it is not what I accomplish that matters most, but who I am that will truly have a lasting impact here and hereafter. Wes, together with Jim Barnes, President of Indiana Wesleyan University were actually the ones who inspired me to jot down my thoughts relative to the laws of thermodynamics, and their guidance on leadership in the form of this book. If this book helps you, please thank them.

Finally, let me acknowledge Dr. Robert Moeller who counseled me on the book and lent his biblical correctness oversight and editing eye toward the structure of it. He was very helpful.

Acknowledgements would be incomplete without a special thank you to my Administrative Assistants, Julie Rainey and Michelle Kline. These partners worked tirelessly in helping me organize and execute my assignments professionally and personally. Thanks for making it all happen.

To all, be strong and of good courage.

SECTION ONE

CHAPTER 1

The Zeroth Law of Thermodynamics

*E*nergy flows from high to low. This is the essence of the First Law of Thermodynamics, also known as the Zeroth Law. It impacts everything around us from how we cool our sodas in the summer to how we provide effective leadership in a changing world.

How did this important principle of physics and human dynamics get its unusual name -- the "Zeroth Law?" As it happens, the First and Second Laws of Thermodynamics were discovered and named long before scientists discovered that a more fundamental law existed. Therefore, this new law deserved to come in order before the two, yet the names "First Law" and "Second Law" were already taken. The solution? The scientific powers decided to call it the Zeroth Law to avoid confusion (the jury is still out whether they were successful in doing so).

Trivia aside, the Zeroth Law is actually quite simple: it says energy flows from high sources to low sources, and not the other way around. You can think of it like water. Water will flow downhill, from higher ground to lower ground, but you'll never see water flowing back up a hill or waterfall. In similar fashion all forms of energy must flow from their high sources toward lower sources.

I was able to teach the Zeroth Law to my son, Justin, while we were eating dinner one evening. He had abruptly excused himself from the table to walk over to the refrigerator, open the freezer, and put a handful of ice cubes into his glass of soda. When he returned to the table I asked him, "Why did you do that?"

"Why did I put ice in my soda?" He seemed confused that I would even ask such a question. Then it dawned on him: the question was neither purely inquisitive nor rhetorical in nature, but another uninvited teaching moment barreling straight down on him (it has not been easy growing up in my home).

"Dad, I like my pop cold," he said in a matter of fact voice.

"I know you like your drinks cold, but why did you put ice in it?"

"Because ice makes it cold," he replied (no doubt wondering how his father ever became a Chief Engineer of the world's largest vehicle platform).

I startled him (and everyone else) when I smacked my hand on the table and said in an authoritative voice, "No, it does not! That ice cannot make the pop cold. That would be a violation of the Zeroth law of thermodynamics. And those laws will not be broken in this house!"

By now I had everyone's attention (even our dog was listening).

"Son," I said in a more conciliatory voice, "The laws of thermodynamics are not just guidelines or suggestions. They are irrefutable laws. God himself spoke them into existence. Remember, sometimes when God speaks he speaks in equation!"

By now I think my son was wishing he had drunk his glass of soda lukewarm.

I continued: "What is happening right before your very eyes is that **the soda is making the ice warm, rather then the ice making the pop cold.** That's what the Zeroth Law says must happen. *Energy flows from high sources to low*, so in keeping with that, the soda is making the ice warm up. As it does the soda gives up some of its own energy and as a result the temperature of the soda indeed goes down."

Understanding I had a captive audience there was no reason to stop now.

"In fact, as the soda warms the ice it undergoes a phase change, or a change of state. The ice starts to melt changing from a solid to a liquid. As it changes state it takes in the latent heat of fusion which really absorbs energy from the soda and the temperature falls commensurately."

You can hardly imagine the smile of Socratic contentment on my face and the look of trained patience on my son. "Thanks Dad, I'll be a better man because of this," he offered in return.

And so it is. Energy always flows from higher sources to lower sources or from a greater amount of energy to a lower amount. You may have experienced this when you open the front door of your house on a wintry day and you hear someone else shout, "Close the door! You're letting the cold in."

Now you can set the record straight. I am not "letting the cold in" rather I am "letting the warmth out." Cold air doesn't cause the air to flow rather the warm air does. So while the house gets a little colder because some of the warm air has left, that is only the consequence, not the effect.

Only a strong and fully charged car battery can be used to jump a weaker one rather than the other way around. The electrical energy will flow from the higher potential state of the good battery to the lower potential state of the weaker one. That is the Zeroth law, and it is irrefutable. We would all do well to understand it, and to realize its larger ramifications for our world, our own life, and our ability to lead.

CHAPTER 2

The Zeroth Law of Leadership

One of the truly exciting discoveries of life for me has been that the laws of leadership can also be described by the laws of nature. The laws that govern how we effectively influence and lead people are clearly visible and deeply imbedded in the laws of thermodynamics. What is the study of thermodynamic laws if not the study of energy and power? What is the study of leadership laws if not the study of focused energy and power of certain individuals? As a result it's fair to substitute the word "leadership" when you read the word "energy" in the Laws of Thermodynamics. You'll discover in each case the laws still hold!

That being the case, the Zeroth Law now reads, "*Leadership flows from high to low.*" Leadership, like energy, must always flow from high sources to lower ones, and not the other way around. Stated in another way *true leadership does not flow from the masses.* This is the Law that explains and validates the cliché, "It's all about leadership."

It is common to hear people grouse that their employees or associates are not looking at "the big picture." As a result they are missing a grand opportunity to improve their lot in life or chances for success. If only they would *just do what anybody can see needs to be done.* However, this thought process is flawed because you cannot look to the masses to exert effective leadership anymore than you can look to the ice cube to cool the glass of soda.

Leadership is the focused energy of an individual(s) that is able to communicate a vision for a higher and more preferable state of being. Or to state in another way, leaders are people who have the ability to express a compelling idea that in turn inspires others to focus their efforts in a single direction to achieve a significant objective.

Examples of the Zeroth Law of Leadership abound. From the simple to the most complex situations, energy is always flowing from high to low. Allow me to cite a few examples from my own experience and observations.

Just this morning my wife Shelly and I traveled to a local shopping center. It was a bright and sunny wintry day in eastern Michigan. As we finished loading our groceries into our Yukon Denali, I looked around for the right place to deposit our now empty shopping cart. It was my wife who expressed what I was thinking, "They need to get a bag boy out here to pick up these carts. What a mess! They are everywhere!"

It was indeed a mess. As we observed the empty shopping carts randomly discarded throughout the entire parking lot the Zeroth Law was clearly at work. Some carts had been pushed into one of the two "corrals" provided for them. However, where the first ones wheeled into the corral were neatly aligned and nested together, the carts behind them were randomly shoved into the corral area. The result was a terribly inefficient use of space.

Worse than that, a number of carts had simply been left unattended in open parking stalls beside shoppers' vehicles. Patrons who either did not see the corrals or who were too careless to take the time to roll their cart over to the designated areas abandoned them. The fact that these shoppers left the parking lot with one less usable parking space than when they had arrived apparently did not bother them. (This situation is also a vivid picture of the Second Law of Thermodynamics at work, but more on that later.)

Here is where the Zeroth Law of Leadership decides whether a chaotic situation is remedied or not. A store manager who does not understand that energy flows from high to low might be tempted to come out, survey the carts in chaos, and cry out, "What in the world is wrong with these shoppers? Don't they see the nice cart corrals we've provided for them? Don't they know that when they put their carts in the right place the parking lot stays clear, open, convenient, and safe?"

Or the same manager might ask, "Why don't people take a moment when they arrive to push the scattered carts into the corrals as they walk into the store? It would take so little effort and it would help the situation immensely."

From a purely logical perspective, this would make sense, however it would be wrong thinking according to the Zeroth Law of Leadership. *Leadership is never of the masses;* therefore shoppers will never spontaneously organize themselves into a force to correct the problem (regardless of how obvious the solution or simple the solution). Occasionally a few people will move a cart here or there to help the situation, but their efforts will be random or sporadic at best. Left to their own devices the masses will always allow the lot to become increasingly cluttered as time progresses.

> **Leadership is never of the masses.**

Right thinking, according to the Zeroth Law, begins when the manager understands that "it is all about leadership" (actually all about their own personal leadership). A true leader will see the problem as it develops in the parking lot. They will clearly spot the inconvenience, the upset customers, and the potential damaged property and personal accidents that the scattered carts represent. A true leader will take decisive action by directing the bag boys to hustle out into the parking lot, round up all abandoned carts, and herd them back into the store where they once again can serve a useful purpose.

Remember, without leadership operating from high to low the situation will not change. (Note: If the bag boys are well trained and possess budding leadership potential of their own they will police the parking lot all on their own. They can become a source of energy flowing from high to low. We shoppers can only hope their tribe increases!) The Zeroth Law of Leadership posits that leaders should never be amazed that the masses do not lead themselves. Rather they should be amazed if they ever do!

Another case of the Zeroth Law in action occurred when a young engineer stopped by to discuss his career development with me. Many of our younger engineers wish to discuss their careers with me on occasion and I always enjoy the experience. This particular discussion took on a deeper teaching moment than most.

The young man was a recent graduate of Cornell University. He related to me some of his experiences at Cornell as they related to his future at GM. In particular, he was proud of an award winning project he had helped to develop with robotics, utilizing fuzzy logic and artificial intelligence. It sounded fascinating. I then asked him a question that caught him off guard: what was it about his team from Cornell that allowed them to capture first place so handily?

He thought for a moment then offered his answer. Looking back he had been part of a real team, not just a collection of guys wearing the same color jersey, but a real team. They were "the most intelligent students he had ever met or been honored to be associated with." To a person they were each motivated to win, to pull their own weight, and to pursue a common goal.

I could tell that he was pleased with his answer. That's why he was a little taken aback when I looked at him and said, "What you just said cannot be true." He looked at me with an expression somewhere between mystified and confused. (Raising three children had prepared me for his look of bewilderment! Reference the soda pop and ice cubes…)

I explained that the Zeroth Law of Thermodynamics (and hence the same Law of Leadership) would not allow their group to succeed as it did. Even if they had gathered a rare collection of excellent minds, forged them together into a functional team, and agreed on a common objective or goal **they could not achieve greatness**. It would be a fundamental violation of the Zeroth Law and therefore impossible.

I went on to explain that what will happen by nature is that each mind will come up with a method or way to accomplish the goal independent of the others. If their egos happen to be proportionate to their genius, as they often are, they will each blaze the path toward the objective as they think best. The result will be a sub-optimization of the whole at best, and total failure at the worse.

I explained that somewhere along the line, one of these Cornell scholars rose to the task of leadership, and became the higher source of energy. Someone emerged from the group who was able to articulate a vision and a plan and was able to convince the others of its value. Someone was able to motivate all the other members to think, scheme, and create their portion of the robot in a way that was seamlessly integrated into the whole.

Admittedly, it might have been different students playing this role at different times in different areas of responsibility, but they were never without a leader. Even among the best and brightest students, leadership must flow from a higher source to a lower source.

Considering my new paradigm the young engineer was able to think back on the leadership that emerged from the group and acknowledged it was so good that it hardly stood out. It was the application of solid, consistent leadership that allowed their collective genius flourish, and their work lead to a winning effort. Bold or reserved, it's all about leadership and it will always flow from high to low.

Don't get the wrong idea that this "flow of leadership" is always necessarily related to the rank or position of an individual in a group. Although that tends to be the case, leadership is not limited to the hierarchical structure of a business, government, school system, or family. All that the Zeroth Law cares about is the relative position of the focused energy, and it can be found almost anywhere in a structure or organization. Allow me a few examples that hopefully will clarify my point.

Some time ago a very popular movie was released entitled, "The Matrix Reloaded." This was the hit sequel to the original "Matrix" movie staring Keanu Reeves, Carrie Ann Moss and Laurence Fishburne. As popular as this film proved to be with the general public, it proved even more popular within the ranks of General Motors. The primary reason this particular group liked the movie was not necessarily the acting but it was more the automotive stunts executed in the movie they enjoyed. The two vehicles used in the major chase scene (which lasted about eleven minutes) were two of GM's newest entries, the Cadillac Escalade EXT and the Cadillac CTS.

Obviously the marketing types were very pleased (you can hardly buy that kind of exposure). But the engineering folks were equally thrilled to see the fruits of their labors get such dramatic cinematic exposure.

Two engineers who had worked on these vehicles were so impressed by the publicity their division received with this hit movie, were moved to the point of action. They came up with an idea to recognize and reward all those engineers who had worked so hard on these vehicles: take them to an exclusive matinee showing of the movie. They pitched the idea to me, the Chief Engineer of the Escalade, and to the Chief of the CTS. We agreed that they were on to a good idea and we were able to find a few dollars in our budgets to fund the outing. With approval (from higher sources of energy) they were off to the races.

They first recruited a small group of engineers to help them with the event. They then contracted with a local movie theater for a private showing of the film to about 500 engineers. They not only printed tickets to be used as invitations, but also arranged for one of the actual CTS's and Escalades used in the filming to be shipped into the lobby of the theater. Bullet holes and all! They also convinced us Chiefs to dress in Matrix attire complete with sunglasses and long overcoats. Not only that, but they also coerced us to make a pre-show appearance and deliver a rousing speech to the crowd.

It served as a great way to say thank you to so many people for their dedication and efforts. The interesting part of this success story is that it was handled almost entirely by two "level seven" engineers. If you looked at our organizational chart you would never guess that such effective leadership would rise up from the middle of the pack, but it did. They became, at least for this activity, the "higher source of energy" that benefited so many of their peers and friends. *Rank and position do not always predict leadership, but the output of focused energy and efforts always will.* Interesting note: as of this publication, one of these engineers has been promoted several times and is now filling an executive position due to his consistent demonstration of leadership abilities.

Just as rank and position are not always predictors of leadership, neither is age. The Scriptures recognize that, "*a head of silver is a crown of wisdom,*" and so typically the older and more experienced will be the source of wise counsel and leadership to the younger generation. Occasionally, however, this is not true.

Consider the Sunday school student who is running the show, not the teacher in front of the class. Or think of junior high student who is the leader of the pack (ringleader). While they are moving the entire group in a fun direction the instructor is left wondering how they lost control in the first place.

What's happening is quite simple according to the Zeroth Law. A child has risen above his peers, becoming the higher source of energy, and his leadership is flowing downward. As an adult, rather than becoming nonplussed by their success it might be a good idea to keep an eye on such a child for future leadership roles.

How much more our businesses might succeed if we recognized the Zeroth Law of Leadership at work and fanned the flames of leadership in our employees instead of dousing them. Good leaders will choose to guide rather than obstruct such emerging leadership.

Conversely, business too often awards people with elevated positions of leadership that simply do go way beyond their energy to lead. The Zeroth Law will work against this type of promotion and if it is allowed to remain in place it will be at the peril and cost of the business. Your enterprise can achieve greatness by carefully cultivating and exploiting emerging sources of "high energy" as they appear.

How much more could our schools improve if math teachers led their students with the same energy and intensity that a football coach leads his team with? A good coach never allows a player to show up at a game or practice without understanding their assignments as described in their playbook. If it happens there will be hell to pay and laps to run for sure. Yet, all too often a student can wander into a classroom completely unprepared and little is said or done about it by the teacher.

I witnessed a marching band from a local inter-city high school perform at the celebration of one of our assembly plants that had just built its 2,000,000th vehicle. The precision and discipline they displayed marching was remarkable, but it was even more on display when they entered our cafeteria to eat lunch. Their regimented behavior would make the toughest marine drill sergeant proud. You can be certain they do not show up to class without proper preparation. You can also be certain their exemplary behavior is due to the strong leadership of their instructor (who understands the Zeroth Law)!

> It's all about leadership means the responsibility for great leadership rests solely on the shoulders of those willing to invest their energy and work to help those they can influence and motivate to a higher better state of living.

Remember **leadership is energy**. Life itself is the result of harnessing and directing the energy we each possess in our bodies. Leadership is simply harnessing and directing our own energy and that of others toward a common good or goal.

Remember also that energy is directly related to work. Work is force (energy) acting through a distance. **Leadership is work,** work that is difficult and never ceasing. This fact may help explain why so few aspire to and succeed at being great leaders.

It also helps explain why leadership is not of the masses. Masses are reluctant to expend difficult and unceasing energy. When they do try to do so the best they can hope for are mediocrity and the worst -- a riot. Great leadership takes a great amount of work and the average individual is simply unwilling to make that level of sacrifice and effort.

What kind of leader are you? Are you waiting for your employees to pick themselves up by their bootstraps and solve their own problems? Are you amazed they have not done so? Are you looking for the people in your neighborhoods to organize themselves to address problems they face? Are you looking at your students and wondering why they don't "get their acts together"?

Or are you the kind of leader who acknowledges the Zeroth Law of Leadership and understands that leadership flows from higher sources to lower ones? "It's all about leadership" means the responsibility for great leadership rests solely on the shoulders of those willing to invest their energy and work to help those they can influence and motivate to a higher, "better" state of living. Will you be that higher source of leader the zeroth laws demand you to be?

CHAPTER 3

The Zeroth Law of Truth

I am an engineer by genetics, training and choice.

As a result I tend to look at life through the lenses of logic, science and mathematics. As a follower of Jesus Christ I also invest considerable time in the study of the Scriptures to find truth, wisdom and direction for my own life.

When I first became a believer and began to grow in the faith, I often felt as if I had a foot in two separate buckets. One bucket was the natural laws that govern the universe and that are studied in all the sciences. The other bucket was a spiritual one with theological truths that are discovered through study of the Bible.

With time I have come to realize this is not really the case. I have come to appreciate the fact that I have both feet in the same bucket whether I am studying science or the Bible. It is just a much bigger bucket than most people realize. The God who speaks to us through his Word, the Holy Bible, is the same God who speaks to us throughout all of nature and His creation.

God indeed has spoken to us in many ways. He spoke directly with individuals such as Adam, Eve, Abraham and Moses (the latter from a burning bush). At other times He has spoken through his prophets, and still others times through ordinary people. He speaks to us today primarily through His written

Word (theologians call this *special revelation*). We must also remember that He also speaks through nature; we can see His handy work and draw inferences about His character through our observations (theologians call this *general revelation*).

The Bible tells us: *"Christ is the visible image of the invisible God. He existed before God made anything at all and is supreme over all creation. Christ is the one through whom God created everything in heaven and earth. He made the things we can see and the things we can't see – kings, kingdoms, rulers, and authorities. Everything has been created through him and for him. He existed before everything else began, and he holds all creation together"* *(Colossians 1:13-17).*

When God speaks, He sometimes speaks in equations. When He said, *"Let there be light,"* in Genesis 1:14, He also said, "$\Delta (v, \Omega) \equiv 1/\pi \int \Omega (\beta) \exp [\beta (\hat{a}\dagger - v^*) - \beta^*(\hat{a} - v) \, d2 \, \beta$" and there was light!

God is not the author of confusion; the universe obeys His ordained repeatable and observable laws. Christ is the One who commanded these laws into existence when He created everything in the universe. All beings, bodies, and creatures must obey them. Regardless of your rank, power, status, or beliefs, if you step off the roof of a building you will travel downward toward the center of the earth at one "g", -9.8 m/s^2!

I am excited not only to see the laws of nature, and in particular the laws of thermodynamics, played out in business and leadership, I also see them reflected in our spiritual life. The Zeroth Law of Thermodynamics can be seen playing itself out again and again throughout the Scriptures. A few examples may help illustrate the point.

Shortly after the establishment of groups of nations and of peoples recorded in Genesis, we are told that all went their own way spiritually and forgot about the God who had made them.

In their overweening pride they attempted to build towers and cities to provide the security that only God could truly offer.

Although people were able to see that there was a great Creator who had fashioned "the invisible things of the earth," they could not lead themselves back to a healthy relationship with their Creator. This attempt to build their own towers and security aroused God's indignation.

The Bible tells us, *"But God shows his anger from heaven against all sinful, wicked people who push the truth away from themselves. For the truth about God is known to them instinctively. God has put this knowledge in their hearts. From the time the world was created, people have seen the earth and sky and all that God made. They can clearly see his invisible qualities – his eternal power and divine nature. So they have no excuse whatsoever for not knowing God"* (Romans 1:18-20).

God decided to raise-up a leader, one who would lead a nation of special people back to a loving and intimate relationship with Himself. That man was named Abraham. God said to him, *"Leave your country, your relatives, and your father's house, and go to the land that I will show you. I will cause you to become the father of a great nation. I will bless you and make you famous, and I will make you a blessing to others"* (Genesis 12:1-2). As the Zeroth Law of Leadership predicts, the masses were not able to lead themselves back to God; it required the Lord Almighty to provide the higher source of energy to do so (in the person of a leader).

He did this again several times as recorded in Scripture. Egypt enslaved this special nation of Abraham for nearly 400 years. God heard their cries of pain and anguish and was moved to intercede. He commissioned a leader for the job of liberating them, a man named Moses. He spoke to Moses, *"Now go, for I am sending you to Pharaoh. You will lead my people, the Israelites out of Egypt"* (Exodus 3:10).

Following another span of history we again find God looking for a leader. It appeared that his chosen people were incapable of leading themselves and continued to fall away from Him. They had once again turned to their own ways and desires. God expressed His distress when He called out, *"Whom shall I send as a messenger to my people? Who will go for us?"*

Thankfully, there was a person willing to become the higher source of energy and leadership, the man Isaiah, son of Amoz. He humbly responded, *"Lord, I'll go. Send me" (Isaiah 6:8)*. Isaiah was used of God to bring the Lord's people to a better spiritual place.

The ultimate example of the Zeroth Law of Leadership in action is found in Jesus Christ Himself. During his days on earth He looked at the people and wept as he saw their great need to be reconciled to the Father. He was moved by their need to regain the precious relationship that they were created for, but unable to obtain on their own. They not only needed a leader, they needed the Ultimate Leader (the Hebrew concept of a Messiah) for a task of this magnitude.

Jesus was that needed leader come to earth. He said, *"I am the way, the truth and the life. No one comes to the Father, except through Me."* Again he said, *"Come follow me."* This proved not just a command for a few special disciples, but rather a universal command for all mankind. He validated these directives through his teachings, with his life, and ultimately with his death and resurrection.

Again, the Zeroth Law helps us understand our spiritual condition. The masses are incapable of saving themselves. Try as we might to balance the scales of our wrongs, sinful deeds, shameful acts and unworthy thoughts by doing good and righteous acts, we will always fall desperately short. God regards our human efforts at righteousness as "filthy rags" in his eyes. We cannot balance the scales of good and bad on our own.

That is why we need a Leader not only to show us the way, but to make the way for each of us. Jesus did that for us on the cross. He told us that if we place our trust in him and his leadership, we can be forgiven of all our sins. As he explained to the scholarly Jewish leader Nicodemus, *"For God so loved the world that he gave his one and only Son, that whoever believes in him shall not perish but have eternal life" (John 3:16).*

Listen also to the words spoken by the prophet Isaiah nearly 750 years before Christ's sacrifice of His own life on the Cross at Calvary: *"Who has believed our message? To whom will the Lord reveal his saving power? My servant (Jesus) grew up in the Lord's presence like a tender green shoot, sprouting from a root in dry and sterile ground. There was nothing beautiful or majestic about his appearance, nothing to attract us to him. He was despised and rejected – a man of sorrows, acquainted with bitterest grief. We turned our backs on him and looked the other way when he went by. He was despised, and we did not care.*

Yet it was our weaknesses he carried; it was our sorrows that weighted him down. And we thought his troubles were a punishment from God for his own sins! But he was wounded and crushed for our sins. He was whipped, and we were healed! All of us have strayed away like sheep. We have left God's paths to follow our own. Yet the Lord laid on him the guilt of sins of us all.

He was oppressed and treated harshly. Yet he never said a word. He was led like a lamb to the slaughter. And as a sheep is silent before the shearers, he did not open his mouth. From prison and trial they led him away to his death. But who among the people realized that he was dying for their sins – that he was suffering their punishment? He has done no wrong, and he never deceived anyone. But he was buried like a criminal; he was put in a rich man's grave.

But it was the Lord's good plan to crush him and fill him with grief. Yet when his life is made an offering for sin, he will have a multitude of children, many heirs. He will enjoy a long life, and the lord's plan will prosper in his hands. When he sees all that is accomplished by his anguish, he will be satisfied. And because of what he has experienced, my righteous servant will make it possible for many to be counted righteous.

For he will bear all their sins. I will give him the honors of one who is mighty and great, because he exposed himself to death. He was counted among those who were sinners. He bore the sins of many and interceded for sinners" (Isaiah 53: 1-12).

The Apostle Paul clarified this prophetic message when he wrote to the Roman church. He resounds with the Good News. He tells us that although, *"we have all sinned and fall short of God's glorious standard,"* and that *"the wages of sin is death,"* there is hope, *"The free gift of God is eternal life through Christ Jesus our Lord."* This gracious gift of salvation is available to all that would believe.

Now that is good news! That's the gospel message of Christ. It is the ultimate illustration of the Zeroth Law of Leadership in action: Leadership flows from high to low – from a holy God to sinful humanity. It surely did in this case!

Today Christians are called to be Jesus' disciples. We are to lead lives that are pleasing to God and obey his commands. Our lives are meant to have an impact on this world for Christ and to be at His service to expand His kingdom. This will never occur without effective leadership. The primary source of our leadership is God's Holy Spirit living in us. He will direct our leadership decisions to accomplish all the tasks He will lay out before us.

The church is at a difficult crossroads in the world. It seems to be suffering from a leadership problem of crisis proportions. The need for strong and wise leadership has never been more critical than it is today. It is the responsibility of every Elder, Pastor, Teacher and Missionary to be aware of the need for effective leadership if the church is to have the impact on a lost and condemned world that God intends for it to have.

Why is there such a crying need for leaders? Look at the world we live in. Too many people are dying of AIDS, the leprosy of our age. Too many suffer at the hands of ruthless dictators and brutal rebels. Too many abandoned women and fatherless children are left to fend for themselves in our cities, often living as marginalized outcasts. Too many of our teenagers are captured by drugs, alcohol and premarital sex at the expense of their future and even their life. Their need to know a loving God is great. Their need for a caring and involved Church is great. They need leaders who will respond to their pain and suffering.

In summary I submit this point. The mantle of leadership is heavy. It is not to be placed on weak shoulders. If it is placed upon yours, you must be strong and of good courage. Yet, be assured you do not bear that burden alone. Christ has promised unending energy to those who serve Him, *"But you will receive power when the Holy Spirit comes on you; and you will be my witnesses in Jerusalem, and in all Judea and Samaria, and to the ends of the earth" (Acts 1:8).*

Divine energy is available to flow from High to low – are you ready to receive it and lead?

SECTION TWO

CHAPTER 4

The First Law of Thermodynamics

The Second Law of Thermodynamics is in reality called the "First Law." This is because it was the first of the three laws to be discovered and published. Like the Zeroth Law, the First Law is actually quite simple when understood in context, *"You cannot create, or destroy energy."*

That's it.

We do not have the ability to create or destroy the energy that is available to us in the universe. While this may sound simple on the surface, the Law carries with it serious ramifications. It means that we are limited to what is here; we cannot make any more of it, nor can we get rid of it either. On the other hand, we can find comfort in the fact that what is here is going to stay here – for as long as time endures. It is really quite amazing when you think about it: energy, though it may be dissipated in countless ways, is indestructible.

This may seem confusing to those who believe we "consume" energy all the time. If you drive an automobile you realize you must continue to put large quantities of gasoline into the tank to keep it going. If you own or rent a home you must pay electric bills to "burn" lights, gas bills to "fire" the furnace, and other costs to cool the air and cook your food. It would seem we are consuming energy all the time, so how is it that the First Law states that we can not?

The explanation lies in this simple fact: we are never actually "consuming" energy, we are instead simply converting it from one form to another. While we are not allowed to create or destroy energy, we are allowed to change it from one form to another pretty much as we please.

To illustrate the physics of the First Law let's look at what happens in a typical "energy consuming" situation. Imagine that you are driving a 3000 lb. sports car, say a corvette for example down the highway at 60 miles per hour. It took considerable amounts of energy to get your sleek vehicle up to a comfortable cruising speed (Newton's Laws play a part in this too, but we don't have time for that discussion). You glance down at the instrument panel and it appears you are consuming energy as the gas gauge falls. What's happened is you have simply converted some of the chemical energy stored in the gasoline into kinetic energy, the energy of motion by it's engine.

Most recognize that there is a considerable amount of energy locked into a full tank of gasoline, that's why we avoid at all costs the possibility of igniting the fuel outside the confines of an internal combustion engine. Now that energy is being converted to the energy of motion.

Once the vehicle is moving it possesses an amount of kinetic energy equal to one half of its mass multiplied by the square of its velocity. That is, K.E. = ½ m (V) ^{2}. While enjoying the top down and the wind in your hair, the amount of kinetic energy the car has at this moment is described as about 486 kilo Joules of energy. If a careful analysis of the energy burned with the gasoline you used were conducted, you would find 486kJ of chemical energy was converted into 486kJ of kinetic energy. Now imagine that without warning, a beautiful deer steps out on to the road directly ahead of you. You slam the brake pedal and the brakes are suddenly applied to stop the motion of the car. The brake pads press tightly against the metal brake rotors and immediately a large amount of friction is created. This action will arrest the forward motion of the vehicle (and send your coffee cup flying) and in the process of slowing the vehicle will heat the brakes to extremely high temperatures. If the brakes are applied until the vehicle comes to a complete stop (just in time to watch the carefree deer scamper back into the woods), the brakes will have generated exactly – you guessed it -- 486 kJ of heat.

Your beautiful corvette has gone from zero mph, to sixty mph and back to zero. You started with 486 kJ of chemical energy in your gasoline; you converted it to 486 kJ of Kinetic Energy and then ended up with 486 kJ of Heat. For simplicity sake we will not mention heat rejected by the engine, air molecule disturbance or other frictional and parasitic forces such as tire rolling resistance. Suffice to say you account for all of them in the original amount of chemical energy. Nothing created, nothing destroyed.

The First Law of Thermodynamics is always a zero sum game. You did not create the energy in making the car go, and you did not destroy it when you hit the anti-lock breaks and the car came to a smooth and dramatic halt (credit our engineers with the latter result). All you did in your breath-taking ride up the coast is change energy from one form to another.

The First Law demands, "The best you can do is break even!" That's exactly what happened with you and your sports car (of course there is also the amount of pleasure you enjoy form your ride, and the envy you have generated from other drivers of lesser cars, but that's for another discussion too).

When I was in High School, I was a Co-Captain on our track team. My favorite event was the pole vault. I was fairly good at it and usually enjoyed the ride (and imagined myself looking pretty cool doing it). Hard as I trained though, I eventually hit a plateau I could not surpass. I had reached my maximum height and I was stuck there. I remember feeling a bit skeptical when my coach informed that if I wanted to go higher I was going to need to run faster down the runway.

I did not believe him. "All I need is a better pole, or refine my initial vertical take-off jump," I thought. "What in the world does horizontal running speed have to do with my vertical flight?"

It turns out that my track coach was right – he had the First Law of Thermodynamics on his side. In order to increase the maximum height of my vault, I needed to increase my potential energy at the apex of my vault. At the very instant that I stopped traveling upward and transitioned to a downward direction, my Potential Energy would be at it's highest value, equal to my body mass multiplied by my height from the ground and by the constant of gravity, or P.E. = $(m)(g)(h)$.

Let me see if I can make that simpler than it sounds. I needed to vault higher. The higher I flew, the more potential energy I would have at the top of my vault. Everything else was fixed and could not be changed -- including my body mass and the constant of the gravity. (By the way, if your body mass changes during the vault something has gone seriously wrong).

Since the first law says energy cannot be created or destroyed, in order for my Potential Energy to increase, my Kinetic Energy needed to go up. That meant I needed more velocity on the runway (the need for speed). My horizontal KE would become my PE, and once I cleared the bar (to the wild cheers of hundreds in the stands) my PE would once again become my KE as I would fall gracefully into the landing pit. Nothing created, nothing destroyed -- just a conversion from one form of energy to another and from one direction to another.

Albert Einstein advanced this Law to a further degree when he related mass and energy. He stated that they really are the same things, equated by the relativity expression of $E = mC^2$, or energy is equal to the mass of an object multiplied by the speed of light squared. This does not change the First Law it just ties mass or matter to it along with energy. So the stuff (matter) that makes up both gasoline and ice cream is here to stay in one form or another. The energy each contains cannot be created or destroyed, it can only be converted.

You may have heard the old adage, "There is no such thing as a free lunch." That is actually a pretty good paraphrase of the First Law. There are times in life when you may feel, "Wow, I got something for free." That happens so rarely and feels so good when it does we want to believe it's true.

The First Law brings us back to the reality that it really didn't happen. Someone, somewhere, paid for that lunch. In corporate America, it is common for a Supplier of a particular good or service to take their client out for a free lunch. As much as you might enjoy the complimentary Cobb Salad or Mahi-Mahis fish filet, you need to remember the cost of that lunch will be covered somehow (typically in the cost of the goods sold). Many businesses have internal policy barring such gratuitous offers, due to this very fact. Remember the only place one can find free cheese is in a trap!

The Zeroth Law states that energy must flow from high sources to lower ones. The First Law states that while it does so the amount of energy remains constant. The same energy that goes into warming the air inside the house during winter will escape when the door is open. Yet, the same amount of energy is still there, it's just now in a different place (outside).

Again, the total amount of energy available to us in our universe is fixed, and regardless of how hard we may try to alter that fact, there is nothing we can do about it. We are completely and absolutely incapable of adding even one single Joule of energy to our world or making a single one disappear.

Poets and philosophers have dreamed and debated if man has any limits beyond his dreams and vision. The answer in the First Law is clear. When it comes to energy, we have indeed found our limit.

CHAPTER 5

The First Law of Leadership

One day my daughter, Jamie, approached me with that certain look of gravity and heartfelt hopefulness that only a 14 year-old can master. "Please Dad," she implored, "can I take a Hip Hop class?" Now Jamie has been taking dancing lessons since she was three years old. In fact, if I could account for all the money we have spent on lessons, shoes, attire, costumes, recitals, transportation and flowers I would likely show a negative cash flow of immense proportions. Yet, she is my daughter (and just between us, she has had me wrapped around her finger since the day she was born).

I did manage to establish a few rules regarding her dancing passions. The first was that regardless of what type of dance she practices she must always practice ballet. I felt it was important she concentrate on ballet as the foundation of dance for its grace and beauty. I wanted her to pay the price of doing the "hard stuff" first then let it pay off in the more "fun" forms of dancing such as tap and jazz.

Another rule I laid down at the beginning of a season was once a class was started, she would not be allowed to quit. She might decide not to take it again, but once she made a commitment to a class and a group they would be able to count on her once recital time arrived. I maintained this rule for all my children regardless of their sport or club endeavors. I wanted to instill the character trait of dependability; never quitting or letting your team mates down.

As a result, my children learned that when they wanted to add a new commitment to their agenda, it would be taken seriously.

I didn't have a big problem allowing her to sign up for the Hip-Hop class (with the minor exception that I did not have a clue what Hip-Hop was). But my wife, privy to more information and knowledge, gave the OK for both the style and schedule. So I said "Yes" to Jamie and for a few moments, basked in the glory of being, "The best Dad in the world!"

Jamie was about to learn a difficult lesson in leadership, and in particular how the First Law of Thermodynamics applies to it.

When she entered High School, her schedule soon became overwhelming. Along with a desire to participate in ballet, tap, jazz, modern, hip-hop, and pointe, she also became a football and basketball cheerleader. As if that were not enough, she joined the Peer Pressure Intervention team at school, remained active in her youth group at church, and participated in several short-term mission projects overseas. Considering her need to study on occasion and "hang out" with her friends, her plate was full.

It was here that she learned a valuable lesson in leadership: *every decision is a commitment of resources*. All decisions must be viewed as committing resources in a particular manner and with a particular time frame. She was learning that when she made a decision to go on a mission trip, or to join a squad, she was in fact committing a portion of the resources of her time and energy (and my money). As the First Law points out, those resources are not limitless. Try as she might, she could not make more time or find more energy. There was a limited supply of both and she needed to learn to allocate them wisely.

This is an invaluable lesson for all leaders. Leaders are called to participate in and directly make multiple decisions each day. Some decisions are small and seemingly insignificant, while others are huge. Either way, whenever a leader makes a decision they have made a commitment of their limited resources needed to carry out that decision. Unfortunately, many leaders do not consciously realize what an important step they have just taken in making a decision.

Consider the automotive company that makes the strategic decision that all of the vehicles that it produces are going to be remarkably "quiet." Their marketing researchers have determined that what automotive customers want more than anything else is a quiet, pleasant, and comfortable ride while they transit back and forth during a hectic day at the office. The company determines that their vehicles will be the quietest vehicles available on the market, and that "quiet" will become their trade mark and product signature. No wind noise, no tire sizzle, no engine noise, just a plush and pleasing sense of peace and comfort. Look out market! This is going to be a winner!

Now consider what happens when the same company, a few years down the road, discovers they have not committed a single resource beyond what they had done before to make their cars "quiet." They have not hired a single Noise and Vibration Engineer or Sound Technician. They have not purchased a single dynamometer, anechoic chamber, microphone or recording devise. They have not changed their materials they engineer the vehicle with or the methods by which they manufacture them.

What are the chances they will succeed in accomplishing this new strategic redirection? It is not possible to accomplish something given nothing. They will make little or no progress in accomplishing their large objective unless they are willing to make a large commitment of their corporate resources.

This truth holds in our personal lives as well. In 1991, I decided to join three other men from my church in a quest to run in the Chicago Marathon held in the fall of each year. Running in a marathon was one of the items on my "Things I have to do Before I Die" list. Looking in the mirror I realized I'd better get at it.

So four of us decided we would work the same training schedule and take our weekly "long run" together. Like all decisions, this required a commitment of my personal resources including my time, energy, and family.

That spring, summer and early fall I ran a total of 900 miles in preparation for the race. Five days a week turned to six, and four mile runs turned to ten. Saturdays found us meeting to run successively longer and longer runs together, peaking at a 22-mile run one Saturday a few weeks prior to the race. The commitment was huge, much bigger than I had ever expected when I entered into the pact.

Like the standard I had set before my children, quitting was not an option. I might decide to never run another race (indeed this was my first and last marathon), but I would not let my partners down. It became clear as I trained that I could not be committed to this task and others at the same time. Though I could think about problems at work while I was running, I could not read reports or books, dictate or write letters, or meet with associates to discuss issues.

Aside from rare synergistic opportunities, when our resources are committed to one decision, they cannot concurrently be committed to another one. The world's best multi-tasking individuals have not yet figured out how to be at two different places at the same time!

So on a moderately cold morning in October of 1991, I stood at the starting line of one of the nation's best marathons. I had prepared to meet my commitment. My partners gave me the "Arnold Swartzenagger" award for having not missed a single workout or mile of training. I was as ready as I was ever going to be.

As the gun went off I ran and ran and ran, mile after mile, check point after checkpoint. I ran through the ethnic villages where people stood outside cheering and playing instruments. I ran past Soldier Field and up the Lake Michigan Coast. Then finally, with parts of my body beginning to revolt and shut down, the finish line at Grant Park came into view. Three hours and thirty five minutes after I had started I crossed the finish line.

One young lady wrapped a space blanket around me. Bless her! A man stepped up and hung a large square-shaped medal with a red, white and blue ribbon around my neck. It almost dropped me to my knees. I quickly found my wife Shelly and fell into her arms weeping. I had done it. I was a marathon runner. To this day that metal hangs in my study -- a reminder of my determination to accomplish difficult tasks. The resources had been committed; the energy needed to accomplish the task stayed high, and the goal was obtained.

That's how it works with the First Law of Leadership.

Last year I determined it was finally time to seriously consider trimming a few (read 20) pounds from my waistline. This decision required I get serious about changing my lifestyle to get it done. This required I make casual running a higher priority and that meals end at the conclusion of dinner time! Without the proper allocation of time to run and strength to stop eating poorly, my weight loss efforts would prove futile. My decision worked and I dropped the weight -- at least for a while (more on that in the next section of the book).

Competitive pressures will routinely drive businesses and institutions to look for ways to cut costs and increase productivity. When done correctly, these pursuits can mean the difference between survival and the demise of a company. Even our economic health as a nation is directly proportional to our productivity.

Leaders must always seek ways to improve efficiency and cut costs. But if these efforts are conducted without considering the impact of the First Law, good intentions quickly can inadvertently lead to perverse actions.

Former Secretary of State Colin Powell is quoted as saying, "Leadership is the art of accomplishing more than the science of management says is possible." A true statement and keen observation made by a truly great leader. There is, however, a real difference between managers and leaders. Managers are paid to manage, to follow the book, and act according to the established procedures. Leaders, however, are paid to devise clever ways to exploit their current situation by eliminating wasteful bureaucracy and non-value added efforts. Such leaders use their influence and power to increase a team's efficiency and effectiveness; they accomplish greater productivity by achieving more with less. Great leaders realize, however, that efficiencies aside, their decisions will result in the dedication of their resources from one place to another.

Many modern-day leaders have forgotten this First Law which states that you cannot create or destroy energy. They forget, to their peril, that when you make a decision you must be willing to commit the appropriate amount of resources to accomplish your goal. They sit in a position of power and influence and ask their people to accomplish something, given nothing.

Thus the old saying that has become more and more a reality in Corporate America, "We the willing, lead by the unknowing, have done so much, for so long, with so little, that we are now qualified to do absolutely anything, given nothing!" This cute photocopy that floats around the office on occasion is actually a sarcastic nod to the First Law of Thermodynamics. It makes light of the frustration and damage the people feel when they are under the influence of this near-sighted style of leadership.

I have encountered this painful dilemma first-hand. During one particularly bad "austerity" period at a former company, I needed to reduce the headcount of my group to save on our structural costs. An engineering department typically looks like an "infinite sink hole of money" to the financial folks, and left uncontrolled, it surely can become one. We were able to manage with less for a time and worked zealously to execute the projects that we had planned for.

However, the quest for quality improvements in our current products heated up to a fever pitch along with a strong desire to reduce warranty expenses. This meant our engineers needed not only to focus on the future products but also to spend considerable time and energy on the remediation of current product issues.

Again, the engineers were able to work with these conflicting demands for a time, but eventually it became impossible. Their attention was always ultimately drawn to the future product work. They were consumed with the grand development and validation efforts required to "work the bugs out" and to bring the product into full volume production. This meant that the actual time available they could devote to current product improvement was not only limited, it was quickly fading to nothing.

This being the case, the quest for better quality and reduced costs did not materialize as hoped. The people involved could be blamed and criticized for the failure; the bottom line was that our people simply could not be in two places at one time. It was not until we re-instituted a "Current Product" group that we were able to deliver great new items to the market and concurrently deliver double-digit quality, warranty and cost reduction improvements on existing products. The gains to the corporation far exceeded the cost of the personnel involved once a decision was made to commit the necessary resources.

Some leaders actually *"command something to be"* and knowingly *"put tension into the system"* yet, purposefully do not allocate the appropriate resources to carry out their commands. They see this is as **"Bold Leadership."** The First Law says that not only is this not bold leadership, left unabated for long it becomes pure foolishness. This style of leadership does not serve those we lead, it only hurts and frustrates them. Our decisions are intended to lead everyone to success. Our decisions are a commitment of resources. If you do one without the other, for whatever noble purposes, you will fail. It will lead to the failure of the decision, the failure of the leadership, and worst of all, the failure of the men and women who are dedicated to achieving the goals set before them.

Why? The Laws of Thermodynamics decree a fiasco under such circumstances. "It is all about leadership," and it all hinges on great leaders who recognize the validity of the First Law at work in their setting and enterprise.

It is often unclear just how much in the way of resources a given decision is going to cost. In a small business or enterprise, or in the case of a simple activity, the total cost can usually be known with some certainty and clarity. In larger businesses, or decisions of greater magnitude, the actual commitment of necessary resources of people's time, money or efforts can only be approximated. The sticking point is that the First Law does not care how complex your business or your decisions are, it simply demands to be obeyed. The winner in leadership is the one who can estimate the best, commit the most accurate amount of resources needed, and is able to adapt as the true needs arise.

The difficulty in accurately defining the amount of resource needed given a particular decision, sometimes leads to the *"command it to be so"* approach. A leader *"low balls"* the resources they allocate in the hopes of driving up efficiency and maximizing productivity. When done well and wisely, this style can indeed work and inspire the best performance of a team.

However, the practitioner of this style needs to be advised that some things simply cannot be "*commanded to be so*" (in particular those things which violate the First Law of Thermodynamics). If you cannot, or will not, commit the resources necessary to complete the tasks you have assigned both your decision and your leadership style is illegitimate.

> **If you cannot, or will not, commit the resources necessary to complete the tasks you have assigned both your decision and your leadership style is illegitimate.**

In fairness a leader should always look for new and clever ways to "beat" the system, that is, to find the most efficient ways to accomplish the tasks set before them. The critical element is to always realize that in the end **it is always a zero sum game**. The First Law says so.

You can not get something for nothing, and there is no such thing as a free lunch. Every decision you make will cost you something.

Invest wisely.

CHAPTER 6

The First Law of Truth

The First Law of Thermodynamics states that you cannot create or destroy energy. Einstein went further and demonstrated you cannot create or destroy mass or energy. Stated in theological terms, the First Law reads, "The LORD, He is God, and you are not." God alone is in the creation business and humanity is simply left to manage its results wisely.

Genesis explains that God created the heavens and the earth and all they contain in the first six days. Then, the Scriptures say He "*rested*." The work was done, and that was all He was going to give us. He looked on the universe and said that it was good and that was the conclusion of the matter. God then turned the stewardship of his creation over to us and instructed us to use it well.

We find God's will for His creation described in the Great Commission. For some familiar with that term, you may be thinking of Matthew, chapter 28, where Jesus commands His followers, "*Go into all the world and preach the Gospel.*" Actually, that is the second, not the first Great Commission found in the Bible.

The first Great Commission is found in Genesis 1:28 where God blessed our fore parents Adam and Eve and commanded, "*Be fruitful and increase in number; fill the earth and subdue it.*

Rule over the fish of the sea and the birds of the air and over every living creature that moves on the ground." Note the commands to *"subdue it,"* and have dominion. This Great Commission has been the Magna Carta of mankind's scientific exploration and progress throughout the ages.

God is saying, *"Here it is – my Universe. I've created it for you. Figure out how it works and use it to serve mankind. I made you in my image. I am creative, now you become creative. I am inquisitive, now you become inquisitive. I have understanding, now commit yourself to the tasks of learning and understanding"* (paraphrase mine). God invites us to take the energy and matter of this world and to use it to lovingly create products, systems and services that serve other people and facilitate their lives.

He tells us that we can dig the ores from the earth and heat and smelt them so that they take the form of beams and shafts. We can make shelters, food harvesters, medical instruments and vehicles for travel and exploration. We are limited only by our vision, imagination, and the fact that we cannot make anymore of what we were given, nor can we make any of it go away. Try as we might to resist the situation, the LORD, He is God, and we are not.

As leaders in the church we need to be aware of the operation of the First Law of Thermodynamics (and the associated First Law of Leadership). Who, more than church leaders, should be acutely aware that God has created all things to bring Him glory and that during our short stay we are to use creation wisely and for His glory? Who should be the better steward of creation's precious resources? The one who knows their Provider and His intended purposes, or the oblivious individual who looks only to exploit the world for their own gain? Time and again the church is called to be good stewards of our Master's resources. This includes all resources: energy, time, money, talents and all of life.

Jesus tells a rather harsh story to illustrate how important good use of His resources is to Him. The story is recorded in Matthew 25: 14-30: *Again, the Kingdom of Heaven can be illustrated by the story of a man going on a trip. He called together his servants and gave them money to invest for him while he was gone. He gave five bags of gold to one, two bags of gold to another, and one bag of gold to the last - dividing it in proportion to their abilities - and then left on his trip. The servant who received the five bags of gold began immediately to invest the money and soon doubled it. The servant with two bags of gold also went right to work and doubled the money. But the servant who received the one bag of gold dug a hole in the ground and hid the master's money for safekeeping.*

After a long time their master returned from his trip and called them to give an account of how they had used his money. The servant to whom he had entrusted the five bags of gold said, "Sir, you gave me five bags of gold to invest, and I have doubled the amount."

"Well done, my good and faithful servant. You have been faithful in handling this small amount, so now I will give you many more responsibilities. Let's celebrate together!"

As the parable continues, the next servant who had received the two bags of gold steps up with his report: *"Sir, you gave me two bags of gold to invest, and I have doubled the amount."* The master said, *"Well done, my good and faithful servant. You have been faithful in handling this small amount, so now I will give you many more responsibilities. Let's celebrate together!"*

Then the servant with the one bag of gold came and said, "Sir, I know you are a hard man, harvesting crops you didn't plant and gathering crops you didn't cultivate. I was afraid I would lose your money, so I hid it in the earth, and here it is." But the master replied, "You wicked and lazy servant! You think I'm a hard man, do you, harvesting crops I didn't plant and gathering crops I didn't cultivate? Well, you should at least have put my money into the bank so I could have some interest. Take the money form this servant and give it to the one with the ten bags of gold.

To those who use well what they are given, even more will be given, *and they will have abundance. But from those who are unfaithful, even what little they have will be taken away. Now throw this useless servant into outer darkness, where there will be weeping and gnashing of teeth.*

Jesus is obviously speaking of greater things than simply bags of money and earthly returns; he is using real life examples to communicate kingdom values. One particular value is crystal clear: be a good steward of the resources He gives you.

In our efforts to be wise stewards we stand the chance of being ridiculed and embarrassed with results that may follow. Jesus said, *"But don't begin before you count the cost. For who would begin construction of a building without first getting estimates and then checking to see if there is enough money to pay the bills? Otherwise, you might complete only the foundation before running out of funds. And then how everyone would laugh at you! They would say, "There's the person who started that building and ran out of money before it was finished!"* Jesus is referring to the spiritual cost of being a disciple, yet again, He uses a helpful analogy. Remember decisions are commitments of resources. If we make a leadership decision without either the access or allocation of the resources necessary to complete the task, we are at risk of becoming the foolish builder described in the verses above!

> **Leaders must always seek the greater good when allocating resources.**

Perhaps the most difficult aspect of the First Law lies in the fact that leaders must always seek the greater good when allocating resources. This was one of the hardest lessons to communicate to my son in preparing him for manhood. I needed to teach him that in all his decisions he would need to diligently seek the "greater good". When we as leaders are required to make decisions, and therefore commit precious kingdom resources, we must have the wisdom and courage to seek the greater good.

I have often said that anyone can choose between good and bad. Those types of decisions rarely make their way far up the leadership hierarchy. But the hardest task of all is to choose between the good, the better, and the best.

This is the dilemma of decisive leadership. When you make a decision you are committing resources in one direction that most likely cannot be committed in another at the same time. The result is **that you will be left with many good things to do, that you will not be able to do**. A leader's responsibility is to understand this truth and discern the best from the better and the good -- then exercise the courage to walk away from the better and the good when necessary. To sacrifice the best for something simply good would be a shame. This discipline is one of the most difficult aspects of leadership and why so many fail at it.

It is not too hard to envision a typical elder board meeting having a conversation something like this: *"Gentlemen, we made our budget last year, and now we have an additional $5,000 left in the bank. You know that we have been meaning to pave our overflow parking lot someday. Just last week I was running a little late for services and ended up having to park in the very back of the overflow lot. It was raining and I forgot just how bad it gets back there. By the time I got inside my shoes were a mess. No wonder people often complain about the parking around here. I think we should use this surplus money to finally get at this problem and pave the lot."*

A general tone of agreement follows as each member recalls the promise they made to "someday" fix the nagging mud problem. Everyone senses that the value of the outcome of the decision to go ahead is good. It will likely make people happier and might even result in more people coming to the church. The timing seems to be as good as it is ever going to get, after all, a $5,000 dollar windfall does not occur every day. There is unanimous agreement that "We ought to do this."

That is, until one of the members of the World Missions Committee counters: *"Paving the lot is a good idea, but I just received an e-mail from one of the missionaries that we support. They have had a terrible fire in their church overseas and they desperately need a new place for their people to gather together to worship. A gift of $5,000 would go a long way toward helping them to meet this immediate and urgent need. Our missionary family lost all their clothing and possessions in the fire. They are in a desperate situation."*

So the leaders are now faced with a decision – a dilemma. They have two wonderful opportunities to commit the same resources to. What they need is the wisdom to discern which would serve the greater good and then the courage to follow through on their choice.

In this case, it may mean continuing to field complaints of dirty shoes and tires and perhaps even lose some of their attendees. Nonetheless, they are faced with a decision and they must commit their precious resources. They can only choose one. They must seek the greater good and move in that direction. Solving such a dilemma is in a nutshell what effective leadership is all about.

Leaders should also be keenly aware of their need to protect and guard the resources that are at their disposal. Paul writes to young pastor Timothy and quotes Moses when he tells him, *"The elders who direct the affairs of the church well are worthy of double honor, especially those whose work is preaching and teaching. For the Scripture says, 'Do not muzzle the ox while it is treading out the grain,' and 'The worker deserves his wages' (1 Timothy 5:17-18; Deuteronomy 25:4; Luke 10:7)."*

As leaders, we must be diligent in remembering virtually everything that we do involves the efforts of people. These are the individuals whose time, money and energy we direct to accomplish our objectives (regardless of how big or small, noble or insignificant our

> **Everything that we do involves the efforts of people.**

objectives are). We are warned not to muzzle the ox as it pulls the plow. If the worker wants to stop and bite a mouthful of grain to maintain his energy to pull, so be it. Much is gained by the strength of the ox.

This is another way of saying that we need to recognize people's efforts. We need to reward them in meaningful ways. A hand on a shoulder that says, "I know what you did. Well done!" will be received like medicine to the soul. The workers who put their shoulder to the wheel time and again must become a central focus of the leader's attention. It is their efforts you will often be discussing as you "make decisions."

Interestingly, the First Law of Thermodynamics has been rocked a few times in recorded history. Cooking oil was once poured from a small pot and filled every jar that could be found in the neighborhood. Flour was continually scooped out of an ordinary container and produced enough bread to feed a prophet and his host family during the length of an entire famine. Jesus apparently created grape juice, sugar and yeast and turned it into the best tasting wine using just ordinary water.

This radical violation of the First Law is illustrated again in Matthew's Gospel: *Jesus called his disciples to him and said, `I have compassion for these people; they have already been with me three days and have nothing to eat. I do not want to send them away hungry, or they may collapse on the way.' His disciples answered,*

"Where could we get enough bread in this remote place to feed such a crowd?"

"How many loaves do you have?" Jesus asked. "Seven," they replied, "and a few small fish." He told the crowd to sit down on the ground. Then he took the seven loaves and the fish, and when he had given thanks, he broke them and gave them to the disciples, and they in turn to the people. They all ate and were satisfied. Afterward the disciples picked up seven basketfuls of broken pieces that were left over. The number of those who ate was four thousand, besides women and children".

The wonder of the miracles can only be fully appreciated when you realize to accomplish them the God at work had to be bigger than the laws of nature. Indeed, He has shown us many times that He alone is the Author of all creation and the Author of the laws that govern it. He is the One who rules the universe, in matter, in energy and in the lives of His greatest creation, His people. He, and He alone, is the only Person with the power to *"command it to be so"* and it is so. He can create something from nothing, and He has. This should cause everyone who understands the Laws of Thermodynamics to marvel.

As we conclude our discussion of the First Law, we would do well to remember that all of the energy that we are dealing with flows from God himself. Perhaps we can see this best when we pry under the tent and take a look at what life will be like when we are finally reconciled with God in heaven. The prophet Isaiah was given a glimpse of heaven and recorded it for us: *"Although you have been forsaken and hated, with no one traveling through, I will make you the everlasting pride and the joy of all generations. You will drink the milk of nations and be nursed at the royal breasts. Then you will know that I, the LORD, am your Savior, your Redeemer, the Mighty One of Jacob. Instead of bronze I will bring you gold, and silver in place of iron.*

Instead of wood I will bring you bronze, and iron in place of stones. I will make peace your governor and righteousness your ruler. No longer will violence be heard in your land nor ruin or destruction within your borders, but you will call your walls Salvation and your gates Praise.

The sun will no more be your light by day, nor will the brightness of the moon shine on you, for the Lord will be your everlasting light, *and your days of sorrow will end. Then will all you people be righteous and they will possess the land forever. They are the shoot I have planted, the work of my hands, for the display of my splendor, the least of you will become a thousand, the smallest a mighty nation. I am the LORD; in its time I will do this swiftly"* (Isaiah 60:15-22).

On earth our primary source for energy is the sun. Its energy nourishes plant life and therefore causes all animal life to flourish and grow. We, in turn, consume these plants and animals and gather from them our energy and strength for life. Once we are home in heaven that source of life-giving energy will no longer be the shining sun in the sky, but the brilliant energy that radiates from God himself, and from his Son, directed by his Spirit.

And it will be good.

SECTION THREE

CHAPTER 7

The Second Law of Thermodynamics

We now come to the Mother of all Thermodynamic Laws – and this is the big one. The Second Law of Thermodynamics states, *"In a closed system, entropy must increase."* Only seven words, but the concept is huge and so are the ramifications. Another way to think about entropy is to substitute the words "confusion" or "disorder" with the word "entropy." That being understood, the Second Law would read, *"In a closed system, the amount of confusion or disorder of a closed system must increase."* This is true not only in the realm of physics, but communicates the nature of all closed systems.

Let me begin with a simple illustration of the operation of entropy (or disorder) in our every day lives. Our youngest daughter, Jenna, is more organized and tidy than the average child. As a toddler she would often entertain herself by taking her toys and lining them up in a row (I believe there is a clinical term for this but it has never manifested itself as a problem, so we let it go...) She grew up appreciating that her stuff was organized and in control. However the Second Law of Thermodynamics applies to her life as well as any other closed system.

Let's use the condition of her bedroom as an example. My wife often works with Jenna to police her bedroom. Together they arm themselves with a vacuum cleaner, dust clothes, and generous amounts of elbow grease. Their usual plan of attack is straightforward: toys are put away on their respective shelves, clothes are hung up in the closet, fresh linens are stretched out on the bed, books are re-shelved on the walls, dirty clothes are deposited in laundry baskets, and that miscellaneous dish, cup and bowl that made its way up the stairs is returned to their natural habitat in the kitchen. A final mopping up action consists of vacuuming the room and dusting the furniture. It is done -- a picture perfect room worthy of the front cover of Better Homes and Gardens.

However the ever-present forces of entropy are not to be denied. Shortly after the room is clean, Jenna's friend who lives next door comes over to play. As usual they run upstairs to her bedroom and shut the door. The Second Law is now fully unleashed. An hour later we walk up to inform the girls that it is time for dinner and playtime is over. Can you imagine the stunned look on my wife's face as she returns and scans the room? What was an orderly and pristine environment just 60 short minutes ago is now a scene of Bedlam and fright. The toys are scattered all over the room -- some even broken. Neatly arranged books have been pulled off the shelf for use as trusses and walls in Barbie's latest condo. The scattering of clothes suggest the girls tried on a variety of costumes for a new dance they choreographed all by themselves.

My wife wonders aloud, "What happened?" I put my arm around her and softly say, "Sweetheart, the Second Law of Thermodynamics has been obeyed". The room constitutes a closed system and as must be the case, entropy, or disorder, has increased. I'm tempted to tell my wife that she should be far more surprised if the room stays orderly than if it disintegrates, but I wisely bite my tongue. Instead, I instruct the girls and tell them entropy is not their friend, nor is it their mother at the moment, so for the sake of peace hurry and pick up the room before dinner!

In the previous two Laws we have treated all forms of energy as being equal in every way. Actually, that is not the case. Different kinds of energy have different levels of usefulness. Another way to express the same idea is that entropy is the measure of the amount of energy contained in a system that cannot be converted into mechanical work. The more entropy a particular form of energy contains, the less useful it is. To simplify the concept to its lowest level -- entropy is not your friend!

Consider a hot new red sports car (our previous hypothetical corvette will do). Chemical energy in the gasoline is converted to propel the vehicle down the road at 60 miles per hour (okay, maybe 80). That same energy is then converted into mechanical energy or kinetic energy.

When our wayward deer unexpectedly crossing the road we apply the anti-lock disc brakes that completely arrests the forward motion of the car. We have not only successfully spared the graceful deer from an untimely ending, but we have converted the vehicle's kinetic energy into heat energy released at the point of the brake pads. Now remember, according to the First Law of Thermodynamics, no energy was gained or lost in this demonstration of skid mark respect for all creatures great and small. The amount of energy released during each of these conversions is exactly the same as when we began this tire-squealing episode. It was converted from chemical to kinetic to heat energy with no loss or gain of energy. However, and this is where the Second law enters in, its entropy dramatically increased at each moment of conversion.

How did this occur? It's really rather simple. The ability to convert chemical energy into mechanical work was greater with the burning of gasoline than with the kinetic energy released by movement of the car forward. Yet the kinetic energy of the moving car had a much greater ability to be converted into mechanical work than did the heat energy released by the brakes.

Or think of the Second Law this way. We can easily burn gasoline to make a car move down the highway and we can easily bring it to a stop by generating heat at the brakes. But because of entropy, no matter how hot we make a set of brake pads while it is sitting still, we can not make the car begin to move down the road again. Nor can we then stop the car and by doing so create a tank full of gasoline in the process. The Second Law compels us to use energy in such a way that entropy increases each time it is converted.

The energy in a closed system must flow in such a fashion as to continually reduce its ultimate usefulness to do work. The First Law suggests that "the best you can do is break even." The Second Law follows up and says, "And you can't even do that".

This is a rather sobering concept because it says that we are quite limited on how we can use energy, how it flows, and how useful it is. With these helpful illustrations in mind, perhaps the wording of the Second Law may be more easily understood. The Second Law begins with the expression, "*In a closed system...*" A system represents any set of things that are connected in such a way that they compose a unity or whole. A system can be big or small, simple or complex, but in the end its parts must compose a unity of some kind.

For example, outside the window of my study hangs a bird feeder filled with a premium mix of sunflower seeds and grains. It dangles from a decorative wrought iron stand perched on the ground. These individual parts – the mix of seeds, the wrought iron stand, and the plastic components of the feeder are all related in such a way as to comprise a "system" for feeding the songbirds (and an occasional bandit squirrel). The birdfeeder is a relatively simple system.

On the other hand, we all live within systems that are incredibly large and complex such as our "Solar System". The solar system is a collection of individual components such as planets that orbit our sun: Mercury, Venus, Earth, Mars and extending all the way out to Pluto. I for one think it unconscionable to strip Pluto of it's planet status on the whim of a few discontented astronomers and will personally continue to grant this little rock it's full planet status! Our system also includes untold billions of bits of cosmic dust and debris that circle between the planets. We humans, who inhabit the only planet in the system that can sustain life, are also parts of this grand cosmic system.

"*A closed system*" simply means the system itself is not gaining or losing any of its contents. A working automobile is intended to be a closed system. However, if its muffler drops off while driving down the road the system has been changed. Left unattended by the owner, the new (but not improved) system has been redefined. It is now a louder automobile sans one muffler. "*Closed*" in its simplest form means nothing comes in and nothing goes out.

We have already considered the meaning of "entropy" at some length. In the simplest of terms "*entropy*" can be thought of as the "usefulness" of energy. Well-organized energy can accomplish a great deal – such as the gasoline burned in the finest automobiles built in the world. Poorly organized energy usually accomplishes far less. Consider the usefulness of a smoldering fire at a garbage dump. Energy is being released by the chemical conversion of the rubbish – yet not in any particularly useful way.

The Second Law prevents higher forms of entropy energy from being reduced into lower, more useful forms (which is one compelling argument against evolution as an organizing theory for the existence of the universe – how does disorganized matter organize itself into useful matter?). Energy can not become more useful by itself. In a closed system energy will flow one way but not the other. It is a shame because life would be so much easier if it would.

The Second Law can also be understood when we reconsider the shopping center parking lot with carts strewn about in a random fashion. The Zeroth Law stated that because energy flows from high to low, people will not gather up the carts and create a more orderly parking lot even though this would be to everyone's benefit. Rather, because energy flows from high to low the masses will simply leave them scattered as they are for posterity – to do otherwise would be to violate the Zeroth Law.

The Second Law also comes into play in the parking lot. We should not be surprised that the people do not put their shopping carts in the cart corral rather, because things flow from a state of organization to disorganization, this can be predicted. The Second Law says that over the long haul because the parking lot is a closed system, it must tend toward a state of disorder not the other way around.

This same scenario occurs in all of life. Consider the couple that moves into their first "brand new" house. They have saved for years to finance their dream house and have endured the exhausting mortgage application and approval process. They have patiently worked with architects, builders, decorators and landscapers. They have sacrificed and worked diligently for this moment.

With keys to the front door in hand they walk up the new cement sidewalk and are promptly greeted by – the Second Law of Thermodynamics. As hard as they have worked, and as much as they have sacrificed, their brand new house has already initiated its inevitable march toward confusion and disorder.

How? As the years pass by the sun continues to bake the shingles on the roof. Eventually their edges curl and the asphalt base cracks to the point of allowing rain to seep through. The caulking that seals the windows and doors becomes brittle and loses its natural elasticity, (via a nasty process referred to as post vulcanization). Longitudinal cracks develop and the wind and other elements start to leak through. The glass in the window panes continues to "flow" or "run" due to the fact that glass is actually a super fluid and not a solid. The glass becomes thicker at the bottom than at the top and continues to distort until it finally is unable to stand up under its own weight. Eventually the windows crack near their top edge and shatter.

The paint on the house fades and blisters and then peels away from the parent material is was intended to cover and protect. Their beautiful dream house, from the day the couple signed the mortgage agreement, was on an inevitable journey back into the ground from which it came. It seems unfair, but it is the Second Law.

Our businesses and churches are not exempt from the Second Law either. Though we write mission statements, initiate policies and develop processes with great conviction and insights, entropy must be reckoned with. Confusion and disorder wait at the door to replace vision and discipline from the moment the ink (or toner) is dry on the corporate business plan.

To run an effective engineering organization is a difficult task, and there are few places where is this truer than at General Motors. The efforts and energy of thousands of engineers must be channeled, guided and directed in such a way as to design and develop the finest automobiles in the world. To make this happen in the right way, focused on the right stuff, and coordinated at the right time is critical to achieving the goals of the company. It is also a daunting task.

GM Engineering has been organized into a single entity, but this is a relatively recent development. In earlier days each division had its own engineering department, and each with its own way of doing things!

In the early 1980's the GM Truck and Coach division was in trouble. The decision was then made to combine it with the Light Duty Truck group of Chevrolet Engineering. The result was the GM Truck and Bus Group. I was a young engineer at the time and so took part in the conversion from the very first day.

As a new entity we weren't exactly welcomed in the facilities we once occupied. Nonetheless, the Truck and Bus Group became a lean and mean operation from the very onset. Resources were few and precious and so it was vital we made full use of everything we had to work with.

One perplexing problem faced by the Chiefs and Directors had to do with management and control. Many of the engineers were working on projects that had not been officially "approved" from a planning, marketing or budget and resource allocation perspective. Thus, each engineer operated somewhat as a free agent, entertaining whatever changes or modifications they or their suppliers might call for. While many of these "special projects" were worthy endeavors, they did not fit into any "big picture" of what we were hoping to accomplish. Unwittingly, they actually became a threat to our ability to manage approved work. The maxim that "the road to hell is paved with good intentions" was certainly true in our case. The free agent mode threatened to capsize our ability to focus on approved projects and produce them with excellence and within budget.

In order to get in front of this situation, and to ensure our lean engineering group could achieve its assigned tasks, the Directors decided to act. They instituted a process referred to as EPN, or the Engineering Project Number. The EPN became the only means whereby actual work on any project could be begun or be completed by any of the engineers. The EPNs were formally approved at an EPP meeting, or the Engineering Project Plan meeting. (You may get the idea that working for GM you really have to get comfortable with TLA's or Three Letter Acronyms! LOL.)

Before an EPN could be approved, all the needed resources to complete the task had to be documented and an agreement reached to commit those resources to that particular project. Once approved, the EPN became the checkbook of sorts, paying the bill for design work to be ordered and completed, prototype parts procured and development tests conducted. Stated another way, without an EPN you were SOL.

Once the EPN process took hold it became the way we at GM Truck did our work. With the discipline of the organization now behind it, no one was allowed to begin any unapproved work. The project work that was authorized now had a method allowing us to track and control it. EPN managers became highly sought after people, and they were either assigned to an existing Engineering Group Manager, or to the person who was being groomed to become one. The process worked so well that the days of the free agent engineer were over for good.

As time passed the General Motors Truck and Bus Group became quite successful, bringing excellent products to the market place at a time when the growth in truck sales was achieving double-digit growth gains. In response to such success, the size of the engineering department and organizational structure grew as well. The GM Truck and Bus Group eventually became the GM North American Truck Platform, and later the General Motors Truck Group. With each name change, certain aspects of the EPN process were changed too. Big picture questions began to emerge. Who should manage the EPNs? How large should they be allowed to become? Should entire vehicles be considered a mega EPN, or should they be broken up into more manageable pieces?

With each new question, and with each new interpretation offered by those in charge at the time, the EPN process began to lose some of its effectiveness. What had once been our strongest process, serving GM well in controlling and managing the work performed, now became top heavy, bureaucratic and irrelevant. As EPN reached the end of its life cycle, it ultimately became a process that demanded that **it** be served. One philosophy I have held dear during my entire time as the Chief Engineer of GM Full Size Trucks is this: the process must serve us; we will refuse to serve the process.

When a process, however effective it was at one time, now gains more strength than the people who are leading it, you can be certain you are heading toward mediocrity at best, and ultimate failure, at worst. When a leader finds him or herself as the servant of the process, rather than the process serving them, it's a clear green light to begin aggressively working to change the process. The process must return to its rightful role of serving its users!

Irreversible entropy had entered the EPN process and therefore it had outlived its usefulness. Worse than simply being outmoded and cumbersome, EPN had actually started inflicting damage on our division. When GM combined all of its engineering groups into the General Motors Engineer Group, the tired and ineffective EPN was officially eliminated. Their new process for managing and controlling work is referred to as the CR/DN (Change Request/Decision Notice) process. We will have to wait and see how long this process survives until the Second Law takes hold...

And so it goes. The very act of engineering confronts the Second Law on a daily basis. Customers demand more and more value from their automobiles. They want more and more quality, reliability and durability, and are unwilling to pay for one extra pound of material to obtain it. With the Second Law as an ever-present threat, engineers are pressed to design components and subsystems to perform for longer and longer periods of time and in multiple environments. I laugh when I hear talk of auto companies purposely building "planned obsolescence" into their products. I can assure you no such thing occurs. Rather, every ounce of GM's engineering was being driven to increase quality to unmatched levels, reduce warranty costs, and to provide the highest reliability possible. Even with such Herculean efforts on their part, the second law always wins in the end.

Please do not get the impression that the Second Law of thermodynamics applies only to physical systems or businesses. It actually applies to human beings as well. After all, what are we but a walking chemical energy plant made up of about $9.00 worth of raw materials and a bucket of water! The Second Law of Thermodynamics therefore applies to every aspect of our existence. As you begin to grow older -- and this may be a statement of the obvious -- you realize you are not getting any younger. Each year I rely on stronger and stronger reading glasses. My 5k and 10k race times get longer each orbit of the earth around the sun. Where I once pole-vaulted to soaring heights in high school and college, I know if I tried the same thing today, the only thing I would achieve is the "sore" and not the height.

I can guarantee each reader that someday you will personify the final and ultimate expression of the Second Law of Thermodynamics, and so will I. Your personal entropy and chaos will reach its highest point, your order and strength will reach its lowest, and like the dream house we spoke of earlier, you will eventually return to the ground from which you came. The Bible refers to this expression of the Second Law as "ashes to ashes." It's a phrase often repeated by clergyman at gravesides.

One unsettling, if not startling implication of the Second Law of Thermodynamics is that it seems to apply to our relationships as well. Yes, even our bonds with others will tend toward higher and higher states of entropy, and more and more confusion and disorder will occur. This applies to not only the personal relationships we love and cherish most, but to our more casual acquaintances. Some of the most misleading and deceptive words ever penned were, "and they lived happily ever after!" Where did such a silly sentiment come from? It obviously did not come from observing the physical laws of energy or the laws of human nature. "And they experienced entropy ever after" is probably closer to the truth.

Consider two young people standing together on their wedding day. In this idyllic scene the two look longingly into each other's eyes and make vows of unending commitment and loyalty. Watching this scene unfold can easily lead to the notion that these two were just "made for each other," therefore they will go forward together down life's journey growing ever closer and happier.

Unfortunately, this rosy scenario is not in keeping with the reality of either the Second Law, or with anthropological or sociological studies of marriage. What rather happens all too often is that the wedded couple grows slowly apart, not closer together. Over time they develop different passions, likes, dislikes and dreams from one another. Unchecked, the process continues allowing the distance between them to increase to the point where they find themselves at great odds with one another.

If their relationship ultimately fractures, it can be quite difficult, if not impossible, to repair. The Second Law has once again inserted itself into life, and two previously loving hearts are now broken in two. The names given to this entropy process are divorce and infidelity.

In summary, in a closed system entropy must increase. It's the law. Even nursery rhymes ultimately come to terms with this truth. When Humpty Dumpty sat on a wall, he possessed a certain amount of potential energy that was equal to his body mass multiplied by the height of the wall and the constant force of gravity. When he had his great fall, he converted every Joule of his energy into kinetic energy on the way down. When he hit bottom it was transformed into heat, light and sound energy associated with the breaking of egg shell. His entropy dramatically increased, and indeed so much so, that all the kings' horses and all the kings' men were not be able to put him back together again. He was at least not in the same shape when he once sat on the wall. As a wise man once sadly said to me, "You can not unscramble an egg."

Now I realize this description of this Second Law can seem bleak and perhaps even depressing. Before you allow entropy to invade your emotions and sink into a mode of complete fatalism, let's look next into the subtle nuances of the Second Law, and how effective leaders exploit the fine print!

CHAPTER 8

The Second Law of Leadership

The second law of thermodynamics can be a discouraging thing at first glance. If entropy, or disorder, is constantly entering into every system on earth then what hope remains for the survival of any organization -- whether it be in business, the church, or our own home? Some individuals, once they grasp the significance of the second law of thermodynamics, are tempted to despair. "Entropy is coming! Entropy is coming! Flee for your life before it finds you!"

Okay, most people might not go that far. Yet, there are those in every setting, whether business, or church, or even in relationship who subconsciously resign themselves to the fact that things will go from bad to worse and there's not much any of us can do about it. The ancient Greeks called them fatalists; today we might call them network television broadcasters.

It is quite true that all things, left to themselves, will naturally move from a state of order to disorder and from organization to chaos. That fact of life makes for a bleak thought unless we delve deeper into the wording of the Second Law. Here, somewhat in the fine print, we find the escape clause all true leaders instinctively know exists.

Recall the specific language of Second Law, "In a *closed* system, entropy must increase." For the sake of argument, let us define a system as any set of separate things that once connected, form a unity or a whole. Your home, your family, your business and your ministries would all fit this definition of a system.

A closed system is therefore one that is entirely self-contained, that is, nothing enters into it, and nothing goes out from it. As we have seen, closed systems are the inevitable victims of entropy. The physical laws of the universe decree it to be so.

However, if one can "open" the previously "closed" system it is often possible to slow down, arrest, or even reverse the process of entropy. This brings us to the central role of effective leaders: to "open" the otherwise "closed" system.

How can a leader effect the seemingly miraculous reversal of the second law of thermodynamics? It is not as difficult as it might sound. An effective leader can "open" a system whenever he or she inserts energy from the outside into the inside. This energy takes a variety of forms but is essentially comprised of wisdom, skill, effort, and resources. Whenever a leader inserts new insights, motivation and other critical elements of success into a closed system, they are "attacking the forces of entropy." Whether the impact takes months, weeks, or even a few minutes to take effect, disorder and confusion will eventually give way to renewed orderliness and understanding. This also is decreed by the Second Law. Whenever the amount of infused energy is greater than the forces of entropy at work in a system, entropy will cease and renewed organization and growth will occur in that system.

> **An effective leader can open a system whenever he or she inserts energy from the outside into the inside.**

Let me say it again: reversing entropy in closed systems is what leadership is all about. It is what keeps organizations alive and functioning. It is what gives previously declining systems a new lease on life. It is how true leaders earn their paychecks.

Consider the impact of the effective leader on entropy at home, such as the scenario of my daughter Jenna's bedroom besieged with increasing disorder. True, the second law would, if left unchallenged, drive her bedroom toward further chaos and disintegration (and our property value steadily downward). Admittedly, there are times in our home when outside energy insertion lapses for a moment and the second law kicks in. All it might take to get things going in the wrong way is for some volleyball equipment to get tossed in the corner or a new Detroit Pistons NBA poster to be left lying on the floor, (I'm not making this stuff up). In a matter of minutes entropy is on the march and the forces of orderliness are in full retreat.

However, entropy has a formidable foe in the person of Jenna's mother. Demonstrating her innate leadership as a parent, she inputs the needed energy to halt the entropy process by reminding Jenna of her responsibility to pick up after herself. She will even expend additional critical energy by assisting our daughter in picking up her room. My contribution of new energy at times takes the form of yelling, "Jenna, get up there and clean your room!" (Hey, it is all energy, and therefore, it all helps.) Without the infusion of our outside energy the room would soon become, and likely, stay a wreck. With our vigilance and consistency however, the room can remain in good order. I am pleased to report that as of this writing entropy is the loser and organization still the victor, but the battle goes on for supremacy over Jenna's otherwise closed domain.

Another example of how effective leadership can reverse entropy is seen in the shopping center parking lot we discussed earlier. As you recall, the primary problem is that left to itself, the parking lot will soon become a wilderness of abandoned and randomly placed shopping carts. Given time it will become useless and uninhabitable in terms of customers seeking a place to safely park their cars or trucks.

The second law, however, posits this scenario does not need to occur. Rather, an outlet store wisely managed by a competent leader will consistently infuse the energy needed to correct the situation. They will commit the appropriate energy in the form of parking lot attendants whose job it is to run out every hour on the hour and collect the randomly placed shopping carts. This manager may even require that the carts be picked up twice an hour during peek periods of business.

A store run by this type of capable leader presents a calm, clean, and inviting image to the consumer. The system is routinely "opened" to insure that a customer enjoys their shopping experience by finding orderly and available parking.

If this leader's style is one of consistent, timely, and focused infusion of organizing energy, it is easy to imagine the inside aisles of the store will also be clean, wide and unobstructed. If we are talking about a grocery store as a system, customers will find the produce fresh, the meat appetizing, the floor polished, the bathrooms spotless, and the window advertisements up to date.

Likewise, a continual infusion of fresh energy can prevent the dream house we envisioned earlier from falling apart. Entropy will challenge the homeowner, but it can be forestalled for a long, long time or for at least as long as he lives there. The owners can replace the roof shingles every fifteen years or so. They can paint the outside exterior of the home. He can pay someone to repave the driveway when it starts to crack.

It is not an uncommon practice to further buttress the opening of the system, that the woman of the house provide her husband with a "honey do list" (re-caulk the bathroom floor, replace the trap under the sink, or waterproof the wood deck). At least this is how it happens at my house. While such energy infusing tasks may make for fewer days at the golf course, they will insure several more years of living in a clean, safe, and attractive home.

It should be noted that if the infusion of energy were only partial, the slowing of entropy would also only be partial. If the husband chooses to complete only a portion of the "honey-do" list, only those items that are fixed or repaired will return to health and usefulness. Therefore leaders should take careful note: it is possible to halt entropy in some areas of a system while allowing it to continue full steam ahead in others. The larger the system, the larger the amount of energy needed to halt entropy. A partial infusion of energy will serve only to slow, not reverse the process of entropy.

In our own home we have attempted to address entropy on all fronts. Though we have lived here for a decade now, we continue to seek out new nick-knacks, novelties, and art to keep the appearance of our home fresh and inviting. We have painted the house several times and refinished the hard wood floors. Now that two of the three children are graduated from college and on their own, we are actually looking forward to replacing some of the furniture that underwent "advanced entropy due to adolescence." Translation -- much of our furniture has fallen apart from years of teenagers and friends hanging all over them! (Leaders please note: teenagers and entropy are frequently allies).

However, even in this case we can reverse the second law by discarding the beaten-up couches, worn out easy chairs, and threadbare floor rugs by replacing them with new items from a furniture showroom. We will simply deposit the old furniture by the street curb and allow the trash haulers to help them find their way to the place where entropy has the final word.

Business

There are few places where the role of leaders in infusing critical energy to reverse entropy process is more important than in the effective management of business.

Successful business leaders instinctively understand that discipline is a form of energy that must be continually infused into their business system. Strict discipline must guide the accounting process, the ordering of needed materials, the processing of raw goods into finished products, and the inventory control methods.

> **Discipline is a form of energy that must be continually infused into their business system.**

This "discipline" energy requires both precision and maintenance to support the profit margins shareholders expect.

The application of the second law is obvious. Without leadership, that is, inserting personal energy into the otherwise closed system; the needed discipline is going to fade to the point of crisis. A recent example of a corporation that chose to ignore the Second Law to its own peril is Enron. Consider asking one of their displaced employees how important good order and discipline is to financial success. Enron was once a leader in the energy field. When discipline was lost, entropy took over, leadership failed to respond, and financial ruin became a certainty.

As a business leader, you have processes, policies, and procedures that serve your business well. It is imperative that you continue to put your personal energy into maintaining them. If you do, they will continue to serve you well. However, if you do not currently have such solid business practices in place, or if you are assuming that processes will continue to be carried out with exact discipline, you are betting against the second law of the thermodynamics of leadership. My prediction is that you will eventually lose your profit margin, then your financial viability, and finally your entire enterprise. Make no mistake about it; business, like ministry or a home is all about leadership.

Remember, if you are waiting for the masses (in this case your employees or shareholders) to infuse the energy needed to forestall the onslaught of entropy in your business, think again. Go back to Section One and reread the Zeroth law. Employees or shareholders will not halt entropy because by nature, they cannot do so. That task is, and always shall be, yours as a leader to perform. I say once again, "It's all about leadership".

I made this same point to a gathering of young engineers at General Motors. I was asked to address the GMEST (the General Motors Engineering Student Team) by the head of their division. Their leader has spent time with me attending a vehicle test ride and had been impacted by what he observed.

My address to their semi-annual meeting began with a question, "What is the single most important aspect of the automotive business? With everything that is involved in the design, engineering and manufacturing of some of the world's great automobiles, which one element stands head and shoulders above the others?"

It was all quiet in the room for a few moments as the best and brightest of our young engineers contemplated the question. A few of the more courageous in the group offered opinions based on their admittedly limited experience, but none answered correctly.

To answer my own question I drew a circle on a white board at the front of the room. "Many great men and women in the business would, without hesitation, answer that the single most important element is the product itself," I said. I turned and wrote the word "Product" inside the circle.

"In real estate they say the three keys to success are location, location, location. In the automotive industry, some say the three keys to success are product, product, and product! If we build the best product available on the market, the world will beat a path to our door!" Many engineers nodded in agreement. After all, they dedicate much of their waking days to the creation of our great automotive products. What else did they expect the Vehicle Chief Engineer of the largest vehicle platform in the world to say? The truck division within General Motors ranked somewhere in the top 25 of the Fortune 500 companies! It stands to reason that I would argue that product must be the single most important aspect of the auto industry.

However, I drew another circle on the white board that slightly overlapped the first. "Some would strongly disagree," I said, "Certain industry leaders would argue that 'process' is the single most important aspect of the business." I turned and wrote the word, "Process".

"The processes that we use to guide our work and efforts are critical," I admitted. Again, more heads nodded in the room. "General Motors has gone to great lengths to organize itself into a matrixed structure to ensure that the best design practices are used on each and every product we produce. Considerable time and energy has been committed to creating and disciplining us to employ the best practices available. Imagine how confusing it would be if each engineer in this room went about his or her business in an individual, haphazard or random fashion. The company would soon be in chaos." No one in the room could disagree.

To further strengthen the point I shared an encounter I had with one of the leaders of Izuzu Engineering. At that time we were cooperatively developing the Duramax diesel engine into our Heavy Duty Pick Up Trucks. The Isuzu engineer and I discussed the various engineering imperatives that the planned engine had to deliver: power, torque, durability, all with unprecedented levels of quiet, smooth and clean operation.

I had asked him how his company could be confident that they could deliver to us such an outstanding product. He responded with a confused expression. It was as if he was saying, "I'm not quite sure I understand your question or why you would even ask it." Finally, with a calm reassurance he said, "Our process will make it so."

"He was dead serious," I explained to the group. "Indeed, in the end he delivered just such an outstanding product to us."

By this point a large number of young engineers were convinced that "process" was the all-important ingredient of business success. To further the point, I shared a comment made by an offshore automotive company executive. He was alleged to have said to one of our employees, "You are staffed with great employees and have only a mediocre process. This is how we will beat you. We will win by staffing our company with average people who will effectively use the power of our great process." His statement drew a concerned response from the students. Perhaps process was the key to building and selling quality automobiles.

It was time to challenge the young men and women further. "Some on the other hand will loudly acclaim that the single most important element of our success lies within our people." I turned and drew a third intersecting circle. I could sense many in the room were thinking, "Oh yeah, people. That's it! They are the most important part of the mix!"

"Make no mistake about it," I said with a definite authority in my voice. "The automotive business is a people business. People dream of and conceptualize the quality cars and trucks we produce. People design, shape, engineer, build and test our products. People ultimately manufacture and assemble our vehicles. People finance these great products and people account for the costs involved. Finally, people buy, sell, and use our products. Without question people are critical!"

Now I had virtually everyone in the group with me. (It is natural for people to believe that they are the single most important factor of any process, hence the engineers were tracking with me quite nicely.)

"Well, now, which is it?" I asked the group. "By now each of you have agreed that at least one circle or the other is the critical element to our industry. Yet, you cannot declare them all equally important. I did not give you that choice. I asked, "What is the *single* most important element of our business." So which one is it?"

The silence in the room was deafening. A public speaker or teacher lives for moments like this -- the pregnant pause. Appealing to their natural competitiveness as engineers I laid out this challenge, "The winner in this room will be the one who finds the sweet spot of achieving each of them at the same time." I colored in the central area of the circles where they all intersected, illustrating the design space of mutuality.

Before anyone could venture an answer I laid aside the challenge. "The common area, while it may seem a good answer, is a little too simplistic, if not altogether unreasonable. How could anyone in a company of our size possibly manage all three of these circles simultaneously? You can verify that at my time at GM we did indeed place serious emphasis on each of these elements. Yet, the 'sweet spot' is not the correct answer. No, you will have to tell me the *single* most important aspect of our business is, or any industry for that matter."

A collective sigh in the room was nearly audible. As a teacher, when you lead people to the place of a hunger for knowledge there must come a feeding time. "As critical and important as each of these dimensions is to the success of business, none are the most important," I explained. I erased the colored intersection and instead drew another circle in the very middle of the triad.

"The single most important aspect of this or of any industry is **leadership**. There is nothing more important. Everything else is secondary." I wrote the word "Leadership" in the center circle.

> **The single most important aspect of this or of any industry is leadership.**

A collective "Ah-hah" now replaced the momentary frustration in trying to answer the riddle. "It is leadership that determines what products we are going to make, how we are going to make them, and when we will bring them into the market. It takes great leaders to know what products will be winners, what appearance and content will fill the needs of the market, and what strategies and resources are needed to rally the organization to the task. Leaders keep the organization focused on the product.

"Leaders also simultaneously decide just which policies the organization will follow, and what processes they will embrace. It is they who understand human nature and know just when to emphasize process and when to give people free reign. Good leaders smoke out foolish or antiquated methods and replace them with more streamlined and relevant workflow. Ultimately, leaders instill the discipline that keeps accepted and best practices working. Then they ask questions to hold people accountable for following a certain process or procedure. If leaders stop asking these questions and insisting on best practices, discipline will quickly begin to fade."

"Without a doubt," I concluded, "leaders additionally face their biggest challenge and responsibility when they choose and place people into the organization. Leaders know how to surround themselves with great people. They recognize natural talents, strengths of skill, and most importantly, strength of character. Leaders hold themselves responsible to recognize and reward their excellent people. They continually challenge those worthy of more responsibility with greater challenges and opportunities and reward them with greater compensation.

"At the same time they also have to have a keen eye to identify the poor performers and underachievers and deal with them as the situation warrants. Leaders teach and train those who need to shore up their skills. They align people within the organization in ways that allows them to utilize their natural talents. And yes, leaders must address those with serious performance issues and character flaws and remove them from the company."

"Process, product and people: they are all three critically important. Yet, they are all subservient to leadership. It is all about leadership!" It was a magical moment as GM's rising stars grasped the critical importance of leadership.

The 3 P's and the Big 4

The focus on leadership was the centerpiece of the Full Size Truck Engineering team at General Motors while I was there. Why? The staff understood that they did not personally design or release a single part or subsystem of any vehicle. Nor do any of them help to bolt together a chassis on the production line at any of their assembly plants. They could easily be considered a financial burden and unnecessary overhead cost to the firm.

However they continued to be employed. Why? Because they provide *value* to the Corporation in the form of **leadership**. We openly admitted that either we provide leadership that "opens" the system and infuses vital "energy" or we should be eliminated as an unnecessary cost. This fact of life motivated us continually to be training and improving ourselves to be the best leaders we could be.

In my former division it was understood that, **our passion is for the product**. We spent considerable hours driving our trucks to ensure they delivered the consumer the greatest value for the lowest cost possible. I loved this part of the job and it is why I became an engineer in the first place. As Chief Engineer I carried the chief passion for our product. My task was to instill the "energy" of leadership into my entire division to create the finest trucks in the industry!

As leaders, we also poured tremendous energy into our **process**. We have several processes that served us well and therefore our leaders were strict and forceful to see that these were adhered to and executed properly. For example, we took great pains to verify the development progress of our power trains and electrical systems. We would often stop and conduct a test ride and evaluate the product development at certain intervals. The hardware and software inside the trucks were to have achieved given levels of completion by certain milestones.

When they meet expectations, we celebrated. When they did not, we reacted. If the program development was falling behind schedule there was real trouble in the camp! You can ask any engineer who has been in that unfortunate position. They will tell you that they do not intend to repeat the same experience twice! We expended great and professionally painful discipline to correct a vehicle development process that has gone awry.

As a leader, perhaps the best part of my job was the opportunity to work along side many of the greatest **people** in the business. We had invested tremendous "energy" in selecting and hiring the finest engineers and leaders imaginable. To a person they were of the finest character, unmatched skill sets, and natural talent you can find in vehicle engineering. This may have been my greatest contribution to General Motors. It was my duty to infuse "energy" into the organization through recognizing and placing quality people into their positions. There is a hidden reward in fulfilling such a task. Being in the presence of great people also serves to infuse new "energy" into my own "closed system." Whenever I am in the presence of great individuals, my hearts pumps a little faster.

The task of infusing new energy into our closed system became a daily concern, and became part of our daily schedule. Our team met every morning at 7:30 a.m. for a half-hour briefing. There was not a fixed agenda for the meeting, rather we engaged in an open round table discussion. We discussed important things going on, the decisions that need to be made, and the overall pulse of the organization. I worked to keep us focused and coordinated as a team. To borrow a biblical metaphor, we infused energy into our organization by "iron sharpening iron." We built mutually productive relationships that kept us all growing and expanding in our effectiveness as leaders. Our efforts to instill new energy and discipline into the organization had reached a place of synergism, where together we were able to offer much more together than we could individually.

Our Bodies

The second law of thermodynamics applies not only to the success of our businesses, homes and organizations, but it is also critical to the health of our human bodies. The bad news needs to be stated up front: your body will ultimately succumb to the power of the second law (need I mention the "d" word?").

Yes, we all face the inevitable fact of our own mortality. Truth is you cannot find a more disorganized system than a box full of dust or an urn full of ashes. The good news is, however, that we can significantly postpone our ultimate entropy through practicing regular exercise, eating a healthy diet, and avoiding certain behaviors.

As busy as your schedule is, to forestall the mischief of the Second Law you must carve out some time for the treadmill, stair-stepper or elliptical trainer. You can pick up weights, ride a bike, or walk through your neighborhood at a brisk pace. If you do so on a consistent basis, the skeletal, respiratory, vascular and musculature systems will respond and reward you with a vigorous fight against entropy. The result will likely be a much longer and healthier life.

Leaders need to pay particular attention to the ongoing struggle with entropy inside their physical bodies. Too often they overtax their physical health with long hours and stressful days. Yet, vigorous physical exercise, say, taking 45 to 60 minutes a day, 3-5 days a week, will help ward off the great strain associated with working toward great ends. You can undo the impact of entropy due to long hours, frequent travel, and hit or miss nutrition. All this exercise also makes for a good transition back into our home (where we often download our stress onto our family unless it's been dissipated through physical exercise).

Small Doses verses Mega Doses

Physical exercise, like any discipline, is best taken in small, continual doses rather than long periods of inaction followed by a few, irregular mega doses of exertion. Though we fall into disorder in small increments, we can also input energy in discrete doses to battle the onslaught of entropy. If you habitually run for forty-five minutes every other day, you can maintain good health for many years. If you wait until you are overweight and out of shape, then suddenly take action by running a long distance as a weekend warrior, you are flirting with both pain and danger.

I discovered this truth the hard way.

I battled a habitual habit for several years then discovered how to habitually overcome it. The problem had started innocently enough. I started working when I was just eight years old. I became a paperboy for the Pontiac Press, route 3314. Sixty-three papers were delivered seven days a week -- rain, shine, or snow. Sixty-three papers are a heavy load for an eight-year-old; in fact I think the papers weighed more than I did!

That paper route was both a good and bad experience. While it taught the value of hard work, it also taught me to work hard. Therein came both the blessing and the bane. With each succeeding job, I tended to try to work harder than anyone else. When I became an executive with General Motors, I started working even harder. I was only thirty-four years old when I became the Assistant Chief of General Motors Full Size Truck Development Organization at the beautiful Milford Proving Ground. There may have been younger executives at the time, but I knew of none. This was my dream job, the chance to really prove what I was made of, and what I could accomplish with my leadership skills.

So I worked and worked and worked. No details of the business escaped my notice. I set the bar unusually high. I demanded excellence from myself and from our team in our truck development engineering activities. I read and re-read each report my engineers composed to insure they were all accurate and written well. I attended every vehicle ride event where performance characteristics such as ride, handling, comfort and sound quality were judged. I flew across the country to visit every test site and assembly plant in my area of expertise. My personal motto was, "Sleep is over rated. There are 24 hours in a day, use them all!"

Even though I was flouting the Second Law in terms of my physical well being, the result was one of the best run engineering organizations at GM. I loved my work and was proud of our division as it grew from just two groups of ten engineers to seven groups of about eighty. If you wanted a quality truck developed, you had come to the right person and place!

There were only two problems with this situation.

Number one, my work habits eventually blossomed into a case of full-blown, self-feeding, death-spiraling workaholism. There was irony in this. While I was forestalling the entropy process in my company, I was hastening it on full-speed within my own body. I was burning through my physical reserve of energy and health at an alarming rate.

This was bad enough, but the second problem is **that workaholism is the only addiction that corporate America applauds**. In fact, it not only applauds it; it promotes it and gives the workaholic even more work to do. That was certainly true in my case. My success at work only led to the further endangerment of my health.

My workaholic lifestyle was rewarded with the opportunity to become the Area Manager of the Paint Shop at the Pontiac East Assembly Plant in Pontiac Michigan. (I later became responsible for the concurrent operation of the Body Shop as well.) At this plant we produced 1,224 Chevrolet Silverados and GMC Sierra Full Size Pick-Ups a day, five days a week. The plant ran three shifts of operation from Monday through Friday.

At this assignment I got the chance to learn the manufacturing side of our business which is a rare and excellent opportunity for a product engineer. It also required extra hours to climb the steep learning curve of manufacturing while simultaneously being held accountable for achieving our production schedules, plant safety, vehicle quality, cost reductions and productivity improvements. What more could a workaholic ask for? This was the ultimate binge with no end in sight.

I met these challenges by working progressively longer and longer hours. Even when I was out of the plant, I was constantly monitoring the production of trucks via a pager system that broadcast our production numbers. There were times when I would wake up at three o'clock in the morning in a sweat and grab for my pager. Squinting in the darkness I could determine how many trucks we had produced thus far into the third shift. While my wife slept peacefully I studied what our quality numbers were and then try to ascertain if we were having any difficulties in making our schedule. If things didn't look right, I jumped out of bed, got dressed, and headed off to the plant to find out what was wrong. Once there I would work to quickly help rectify the situation.

You can probably guess that my relationship with my wife and children started to feel the impact of "relational entropy." As strong as our marriage was, no relationship can stand long with that kind of neglect. There simply isn't enough energy available to anyone to give everything at the office and then try to maintain a healthy home life at the same time. My workaholism started to reduce my effectiveness in other areas. At church I became less and less useful as a leader. I had no time to give to my community or neighbors. Once the death spiral of workaholism gets started, it feeds on itself and spins further and further out of control.

Things got so bad that my wife finally scheduled a one-week vacation for us to the Tropical Island of St. Lucia. It sounded like a great idea, but she asked a special favor of me. She requested that I not bring any work along with us including no phone, no computer nor any access to e-mail. If that wasn't tough enough, she also insisted that I not speak to anyone about GM, or about any aspect of engineering or machinery. She was asking for a seven-day total career blackout. To keep the peace I reluctantly agreed.

Things were going relatively well as she had hoped until the third day of vacation when we went snorkeling off a glass bottom boat. Everyone had returned to the boat following the completion of the dive and was ready to get back to the resort. Their relief suddenly turned to concern when the captain broke the starter mechanism when he tried to start the motor. Remembering my wife's admonition to leave my engineering career back in Michigan, I just sat there and quietly watched as the local "captain" tried in vain to fix a broken component.

My wife does not do well with motion sickness. As we sat there bobbing up and down in the beautiful Caribbean, her color began to take on a more peculiar hue. Finally, she turned to me and almost shouted, "OK, hurry up and fix it!" I immediately stood up and asked my son and his best friend for the strings from their swimming trunks. I tied a large knot on one end of the rope and secured the other end to the center of a snorkel. I wound the newly fashioned rope around the flywheel of the motor, pulled hard with the snorkel and smiled as the engine roared to life. Shelly felt better when we got back on dry ground. I felt better as well having gotten my engineering "fix" for the day!

Workaholism is actually no laughing matter. Fortunately, I had good friends and the love of my family that forced me to look at what I was doing to myself. I spoke with a good friend and professional, Dr. Thomas Clark, who predicted that I would be either insane or dead (or both) in five years if I didn't change my lifestyle. Dr. Clark helped me to understand what my motives were that drove me to this extreme, and then helped me establish some new personal boundaries and habits to help break the death spiral.

I started recovery by limiting myself to not working more than 80 hours a week. That sounds almost funny today, but at the time it was a real stretch for me to call it quits at the 80-hour mark. I managed to do it however, and as it turned out the company did not fail, nor did I lose my job. I was astonished.

After a few weeks, I moved the limit downward to a mere 72 hours per week. I felt as if I was throwing caution to the wind, but I knew just how important it was to get my work habits under control. Imagine my surprise when the company again did not collapse, and my job remained secure. In fact, I was actually feeling physically a bit better and was functioning at a higher and more effective level.

Finally, I set the limit at 60 hours, and again, with the same result. The company faired well and so did my career. I learned to manage my work better, to delegate assignments, and to simply make wiser decisions regarding my time. I became a much better executive as a result of this effort.

Today I can not tell you how many hours I work a week. I just no longer need to count them and monitor myself to the exact hour. I still work very hard and sometimes put in long hours. But I continually remind myself to be cautious and habitually keep certain things in my life that demand I call it quits at appropriate times.

This self-discipline process was the needed infusion of outside energy that kept my body (and my career) from ending in a burning wreckage of misplaced priorities and unrealistic self-expectations. I learned a valuable lesson in leadership: overdone and unrealistic work habits can introduce as much destructive entropy into one's life as do lazy and slothful work habits. The key for leaders is wisdom, understanding and discipline. Fortunately, I arrested this hyperactive form of entropy in my life in just the nick of time.

Relationships

Leaders would do well to remember that all the laws of thermodynamics apply to all areas of your life, including your personal relationships. Relationships are directly affected by the threat of entropy. If you enjoy a good relationship with your spouse or loved ones, continue to work on it! If you ignore it, even for a few days, entropy will treacherously enter in. If not recognized immediately, things can go from good to bad rather quickly. Do not be lulled into thinking that things will just remain as good as they are forever. That only happens in the fairy tales. They will not, and according to the Second Law, they can not.

If you as a leader are in the unfortunate position of having poor relationships with those closest to you, or if you simply wish to take them to a higher plane, then you will need to inject new energy into your personal interactions at an exponential rate. The leader who pours his or her heart and soul into their work at the cost of their most precious relationships is sacrificing the great for only the good. Wise leaders see how foolish that particular trade-off is in life. I recently spoke to one of our Vehicle Program Managers about the state of his relationship with his wife. During the conversation I asked him if he had found it necessary to work hard to gain her admiration when they were dating and he was pursuing her. He naturally agreed that he had. "Then why do you think you can keep her without continuing to work to gain her admiration and love?" This is simply another expression of the second law, and it gave him pause...

Fortunately, today I enjoy a very good relationship with my wife, my children. We place a great deal of value on what it means to be a family. I enjoy this current state of positive relationships because as the leader of my home, I now continually pour considerable amounts of energy into it.

Allow me the luxury of sharing a few examples.

I enjoy an excellent relationship with my wife because we value our marriage and we both continually pour fresh energy into it. Shelly and I often go out on a "date" alone to somewhere we consider special. We prefer a quaint Italian place, "Villa Maria" near our home. It is owned by wonderful people and enjoys a fine wait staff.

It is here that Shelly and I can talk without interruption about our struggles and our dreams for the future. These conversations help infuse energy into our marriage. We may disagree and quarrel on occasion, what married couple does not? Yet, we hold dear to the biblical advice that we should not let the sun go down on our anger. So before it is time to turn in, we try to talk things out, apologize, and seek mutual ground. This, too, is a form of energy infusion. It takes time and work, but the pay-offs are enormous. As a result we have avoided the "relational entropy" that some refer to as separation or even divorce. By paying attention to the Second Law we have been able to guard our marriage and discover the essential intimacy it is all about.

My oldest daughter, Jamie, attended Oakland University; a school located about ten miles from my office. My Administrative Assistant was kind enough to schedule either a lunch or a dinner meeting for us at least once every week since Jamie moved away to school. I cherished these times, and considered them the highlight of my week. This is one way that Jamie and I work on our relationship. It takes time and work, but the "relational entropy" of becoming a stranger to your own child has been avoided.

My oldest son, Justin, went to Grand Valley State University. About once a month I traveled over to the West Side of the state to meet up with him for the weekend. We would go out to eat at a nice restaurant in the Grand Rapids area, and then for the remainder of the time just hang out together. At one University sponsored "Family Weekend", Justin and I ran a 5k race around campus together. We would catch a football game or just walk and talk across the campus green. He has shared with me some of his deepest thoughts and issues, including how to successfully pursue a relationship with various young co-eds.

My son is now a man in his own right, yet he will always be my son. I will have to work my entire life, and so will he, to keep our relationship strong and growing. It takes time and work, but our efforts have stopped the "relational entropy" that long distances can create in relationships. Today we use the excuse of playing an endless series of chess games via email to keep investing the energy in our relationship.

When our youngest, Jenna, was in the ninth grade, she was a whirling dervish in her own universe. Again, my Administrative Assistant helped schedule in some of her basketball and volley-ball games and dance recitals. Whenever possible, I tried to co-ordinate leaving work in time to pick her up from dance class and transport her and her friend's home again. Along the way we would laugh, sing and try to trick each other with riddles.

I occasionally "helped" Jenna with a science project or with homework tutorials. I loved to walk up the stairs at night after she had been tucked into bed to put my own stamp of approval on her safety and well being. If the stuffed animals did a quick puppet show or acrobatic routine, what's the harm? It takes time and work, yet it stops the "relational entropy" of focusing on work and financial goals our society seems to encourage.

We continue to do things together as a family. We spend a two-week vacation together each year at a large cottage on Lake Huron. As the children have grown older, we have had to make room for their spouses, friends and cousins to come along. The costs have gone up considerably, but the memories we have cre-ated will last us all a lifetime, and it has helped to forge a strong bond between us all.

The Key

Leaders need to understand their primary role is to open the systems they are responsible to oversee. They are called to input of needed energy to keep the system strong or even to improve it. Leaders need to do this in their businesses, homes, families, relationships and communities. They understand the essence of two rhetorical questions, "If we don't do it, then who will?" and "If not now, when?"

> **Leaders need to understand their primary role is to open the systems they are responsible to oversee.**

I have found it helpful to keep a symbol of my need to infuse fresh energy into the system I oversee. I discovered this particular symbol when I was a Resident Assistant at Michigan Technological University's Wadsworth Hall. We had about 1500 men living under one roof with way too much homework, snow, and beer for our own good.

During one of my first night rounds as a resident assistant I was called to help break up a fight in the dorm. Instinctively I grabbed a baseball bat that sat in the corner of my room (I loved intramural softball).

I noticed the moment I showed up with the bat the fight broke up and the tempers immediately cooled. When the combatants saw the bat they rightly concluded some real tangible energy was soon headed their way if they did not immediately change their poor behavior. I carried that same bat on my rounds for the remainder of the year. The yearbook picture of our house features my bat in the accompanying silhouette.

When I was the Chief Engineer of GM's Full Size Trucks, I had a similar baseball bat in my office. It was engraved with fighting words to beat one of our toughest competitors. I would occasionally take it with me to a particularly difficult meeting where I had to make a strong point. When people saw the bat, they understood that I was bringing fresh energy -- the power, intensity, and urgency of total commitment I was trying to convey.

They understood that the bat symbolized that as a leader I was committed to challenging the threat of entropy with fresh passion and commitment. They understood that I would do whatever it took as a leader to open our system to new ideas, strategies, and efforts to make our division the best it could be.

Above all, the bat symbolized that I believe it's all about leadership -- because that is the passion of my life.

CHAPTER 9

The Second Law of Truth

I hope that the forbidden fruit of the tree that grew in the center of the Garden of Eden tasted utterly fantastic because it sure has cost all of us a great deal. When our fore-parents, Adam and Eve, ate of the tree of the knowledge of good and evil everything changed, and not for the better.

God had clearly told Adam, *"You may eat from any fruit in the garden, except fruit from the tree of the knowledge of good and evil. If you eat of its fruit, you will surely die."* A clever defense lawyer is often able to find a loophole to clear his clients of wrong doing, but in this case, it was impossible. God was crystal clear in his warning to Adam and Eve, very specific as to which tree they were to avoid, and unmistakable as to what the ramifications would be if they transgressed His law.

But Adam and Eve had an Enemy, one who did not hesitate to try to blur the lines between truth and deception. He said to Eve, *"Really? Did God say that you must not eat any of the fruit of the garden?"* This distortion of God's prohibition was a ploy meant to confuse her and set her up to become a victim to his diabolic scheme.

"*Of course we may eat it,*" the woman told him. "*It's only the fruit from the tree at the center of the garden that we are not allowed to eat. God says we must not eat it or even touch it, or we will die.*" It seems clear to me that Eve understood the situation quite well despite the devil's malevolent tactics.

"*You won't die!*" the serpent replied (and lied) with a hiss. "*God knows that your eyes will be opened when you eat it. You will become just like God, knowing everything, both good and evil.*"

Then the fateful words that changed the history of humanity, "*The woman was convinced. The fruit looked so fresh and delicious, and it would make her so wise! So she ate some of the fruit. She also gave some to her husband, who was with her. Then he ate it, too.*" The ancient Hebrew text state that Adam was "with her" meaning, he was right there by her side. So together they turned their back on God's Word to them and the deed was done. At that same moment their eyes were opened to the fact that they were naked. Little did they understand just how exposed they and all their children after them would become to all the consequences of rebelling against God.

Wait, it gets worse. The narrative goes on to say the next thing they did was to hide when they heard God walking in the garden. When God called out to the two of them, Adam responded that they were hiding because they were naked. "*Who told you that you were naked?*" God asked. The jig was up, the party was over, and the curses upon the human race began.

We are told, "*So the Lord said to the serpent, "Because you have done this, you will be punished. You are singled out from all the domestic and wild animals of the whole earth to be cursed. You will grovel in the dust as long as you live, crawling along on your belly. From now on, you and the woman will be enemies, and your offspring and her offspring will be enemies. He will crush your head, and you will strike his heel.*"

Then he said to the woman, "You will bear children with intense pain and suffering. And though your desire will be for your husband, he will be your master."

And to Adam he said, "Because you listened to your wife and ate the fruit I told you not to eat, I have placed a curse on the ground. All your life you will struggle to scratch a living from it. It will grow thorns and thistles for you, though you will eat of its grains. All your life you will sweat to produce food, until your dying day. Then you will return to the ground from which you came. For you were made from dust, and to the dust you will return."

Then I think God must have added in a low voice, "**From now on, in all closed systems, entropy must increase.**" At least, by implication, the curses that God introduced into the world heralded the dawn of the Second Law of Thermodynamics.

As one reads on in the Bible we witness that the fall of mankind continues to spiral downward into deeper and deeper sin. Bad decisions turn into worse ones, trouble heaps upon trouble, pain is added upon pain, and sin multiplies sin. Even when God separates a special people (the nation of Israel) to show the world the way back to him, they, too, are incapable of walking the straight and narrow way. Everywhere in the Scriptures, on all levels, we see entropy increasing as order turns to disorder and knowledge into confusion.

Surely the Second Law has been in operation and the earth suffers for it to this hour. And it all started one beautiful day in the Garden of Eden with one bite of a forbidden fruit! The Second Law jumps out of the Scriptures time and again, if only one has eyes to see it at work. Here are just a few examples from the Bible, which illustrate that the Second Law lives and rules the heart of mankind as a result of the fall. These selected portions clearly portray that the law of entropy is a constant threat to relationships with God and each other.

Moses and the Golden Calf

Perhaps you are familiar with the ancient story of Moses, the man God used to lead the Israelites out of slavery in Egypt. The bondage of the Israelites began when a young man by the name of Joseph (the one with the multi-colored coat) was sold into slavery in Egypt by his brothers. Later, when Joseph became a high official in Egypt, the remainder of his family joined him there to avoid starvation. For the next 400 years, the Hebrews lived under the severe bondage to the Egyptian Pharaohs.

At last God spoke to Moses, a Hebrew in exile from Egypt, from within a burning bush. God commissioned him to lead his people into a free land they could call their own, a land "flowing with milk and honey". The Book of Exodus chronicles the arguments between Moses and Pharaoh with regard to the release of God's people. Obviously not interested in surrendering his primary labor pool, the Pharaoh refused to release the Hebrew slaves. Each time he did so he suffered a new plague that God sent on him and all of Egypt. This same scenario was repeated ten different times until Pharaoh finally relented and ordered the Israelites to leave Egypt.

So began a long trek for the three million former slaves into the hostile wilderness of the Sinai desert. A trip that should have lasted as little as eleven days from Egypt to the Promised Land stretched out to forty years. God never intended for the people to wander for four decades, but exactly two months into this journey a major outbreak of the Second Law occurred that radically changed the length of their travel itinerary.

It all began when God spoke to Moses and the nation at Mount Sinai. The Lord personally delivered the laws and commands he expected his people to follow and obey. He called Moses up to the mountain for a period of forty-days and nights, and ultimately inscribed for him the Ten Commandments on tablets of stone.

While Moses was up on the mountain the moral order in the camp at the foot of the mountain began to break down. It led to an orgy and near riot.

We read in Exodus 32 that, "When Moses failed to come back down the mountain right away, the people went to Aaron. *"Look,"* *they said, "make us some gods who can lead us. This man Moses, who brought us here from Egypt, has disappeared. We don't know what has happened to him."*

So Aaron said, "Tell your wives and sons and daughters to take off their gold earrings. Then Aaron took the gold, melted it down, and molded and tooled it into the shape of a calf. The people exclaimed, "O Israel, these are the gods who brought you out of Egypt!" The result was the people began to celebrate their new god in a raucous manner. God saw the spiritual meltdown occurring and His anger broke out against them.

"Then the LORD told Moses, "Quick! Go down the mountain! The people you brought from Egypt have defiled themselves. They have already turned from the way I commanded them to live." **Just 40 days!** That's all it took for the people to turn away from God, despite the fact they had personally witnessed miracle after miracle in their deliverance from Egypt.

The law of entropy holds that confusion, disorder and chaos are waiting to break out whenever a system is closed. With Moses out of the picture, and Aaron unwilling to expend the energy of bold leadership, the people quickly descended down nature's road of sin and entropy.

The Temple Falls into Disrepair

While the Israelites in the Sinai desert exemplify the moral results of spiritual entropy, the later story of the neglect of the Temple in Jerusalem illustrates the physical results of spiritual entropy. The building of the Holy Temple in Jerusalem by King David's son, Solomon, some 400 years after the time of Moses, can be found in the books of 1 Kings and 2 Chronicles. There the Temple is described in beautiful detail as a place of incredible majesty and wonder. One can only imagine how breathtaking and awe inspiring it must have been!

Unfortunately the story of the Temple's physical deterioration in the centuries that followed illustrates that the Second Law is no respecter of special persons or places. By the time of King Josiah, only eight years old when he assumes the throne of Israel, the Temple has become a shadow of its former glory. Josiah, though young and inexperienced as a monarch, gets off to a good start due to the wise counsel of an older priest who serves as his mentor. The Bible tells us, *"(Josiah) did what was pleasing in the LORD's sight and followed the example of his ancestor David."*

With all due diligence, Josiah tore down the pagan shrines and disposed of the rival idols to the Temple. After Josiah cleanses the land he turns his attention toward the restoration of the once beautiful Temple:

*"In the eighteenth year of his reign, after he had purified the land and the Temple, Josiah appointed Shaphan son of Azaliah, Maaseiah the governor of Jerusalem, and Joah son of Joahaz, the royal historian, **to repair the Temple of the LORD his God**. They gave Hilkiah the high priest the money that had been collected by the Levites who served as gatekeepers at the Temple of God. The gifts were brought by people from Manasseh, Ephraim, and from all the remnant of Israel, as well as from all Judah, Benjamin, and the people of Jerusalem. He entrusted the money to the men assigned to supervise the restoration the LORD's Temple. Then they paid the workers who did the repairs and renovation. Thus, they hired carpenters and masons and purchased cut stone for the walls and timber for the rafters and beams. **They restored what earlier kings of Judah had allowed the fall into ruin**."*

The last phrase contains the telling words. Josiah had to put concentrated energy, effort, work, and expense into restoring what the previous kings had allowed to fall into ruin. Left alone and neglected, lacking vigilant care and maintenance, the Temple of the Lord had nearly succumbed to the forces of entropy operating in our world. Whatever you consider the temple in your life, whether it's your place you worship, or your physical body where God's Spirit dwells, or something else, it will require that you invest your energy to maintain it. As soon as we begin to ignore the temple the clock is ticking on its ultimate ruin.

Jeremiah's Linen Belt

God uses the action of the Second Law to illustrate another important spiritual truth in the book of Jeremiah. Jeremiah was a prophet who had the seeming misfortune of living during a time when God's anger had reached the boiling point toward his chosen people. For centuries Judah has turned away from following the laws of God, even though their ancestors had once agreed to conscientiously obey each and every one. It goes without saying that nothing good ever comes of turning our back on God and carelessly breaking our promises. To make this point to the people of Judah, God chose to use an object lesson.

Jeremiah tells us what happened, *"This is what the LORD said to me: "Go and buy a linen belt and put it around your waist, but do not wash it." So I bought the belt as the LORD directed me and put it around my waist. Then the LORD gave me another message: "Take the linen belt you are wearing, and go to the Euphrates River. Hide it there in a hole in the rocks." So I went and hid it at the Euphrates as the LORD had instructed me.*

A long time afterward, the LORD said to me, "Go back to the Euphrates and get the linen belt that I told you to hide there."

*So I went to the Euphrates and dug it out of the hole where I had hidden it. But now **it was mildewed and falling apart. The belt was useless.***"

Nothing direct was done to destroy the belt; rather it simply was hidden away, out of reach and sight. God even took the extra precaution of not allowing the belt to be washed or bleached (no "All Temperature Cheer" allowed) to prevent someone from claiming that Jeremiah had chemically attacked the fabric! No, the Second Law was sufficient by itself to do the damage. Over time the belt mildewed and fell apart and became useless simply because it was left alone in the rocks. It had to happen; it was the law of entropy at work.

This was God's point in the experiment. His people had not done the necessary work to remain faithful to him. The leadership had failed to point the people back to God for generations. The result was a nation falling apart like a worthless linen belt that has mildewed and become useless.

"The LORD says: This illustrates how I will rot away the pride of Judah and Jerusalem. These wicked people refuse to listen to me. They stubbornly follow their own desires and worship idols. Therefore, they will become like this linen belt - good for nothing! As a belt clings to a person's waist, so I created Judah and Israel to cling to me," says the LORD. "They were to be my people, my pride, my glory - an honor to my name. But they would not listen to me." And so it **must** go.

When the Cats Away...

Remember that when it comes to combating entropy it's all about leadership. When an effective leader is absent from the scene the state of affairs will rapidly start to deteriorate. Things will go from bad to worse unless a strong presence appears to reverse the entropy at work. An excellent example of this principle is found in the book of Nehemiah.

Nehemiah was a good man and devoted follower of God though he lived much of his life in Babylonian captivity. God had allowed the nation of Babylon to conquer and carry away Judah due to their sins and neglect of God's laws. Nehemiah's personal manner and accomplishments were quite impressive however, because even in captivity, he became the king's cup-bearer (a position of honor and respect). This work also gave him daily access to king Artaxerxes, the ruler of Babylon.

On one occasion the king noticed that Nehemiah was sad and despondent. When asked what was wrong, Nehemiah responded, *"Long live the king! Why shouldn't I be sad? For the city where my ancestors are buried is in ruins, and the gates have been burned down."*

From this brief conversation the king learned that Nehemiah wished to return to Jerusalem to rebuild its wall and infrastructure. The king graciously granted Nehemiah his request and even offered him the provisions he needed to complete the task. The book of Nehemiah chronicles how he returned to Jerusalem and set about the task of rebuilding its walls with passion and intensity. He faced significant obstacles and opposition from those opposed to his project, nonetheless he prevailed. The wall around the city was rebuilt in an astounding 54 days!

Nehemiah then goes about restoring good order to the government and gets the city functioning once again. He then went to work to rebuild the great Temple that was destroyed 70 years earlier by the Babylonians. He commissions Ezra, a godly priest and descendant of Aaron, to retrain the Priests, Levites and people in how to worship their true God.

A man of his word, once he completes his task Nehemiah returns again to serve his king. Again, the king finds favor with this great man and allows him once more to return to his own beloved land. But Nehemiah has been absent from Jerusalem for over a decade. Unfortunately the Second Law of thermodynamics has been at work during his hiatus!

We resume the story in the 13th chapter of the book of Nehemiah. There we find that Eliashib, the head priest of the Temple, has allowed a wicked man, Tobiah, to move in and turn a sacred portion of the Temple into his personal condominium! Nehemiah writes, *"I was not in Jerusalem at that time, for I had returned to the king in the thirty-second year of the reign of king Artaxerxes of Babylon, though I later received his permission to return. When I arrived back in Jerusalem and **learned the extent of this evil deed** of Eliashib - that he had provided Tobiah with a room in the courtyards of the Temple of God - I became very upset and threw all of Tobiah's belongings from the room. Then I demanded that the rooms be purified, and I brought back the utensils for God's Temple, the grain offerings, and the frankincense.*

*I also discovered that the Levites had not been given what was due them, so they and the singers who were to conduct the worship services had all returned to work their fields. I immediately confronted the leaders and demanded, **"Why has the Temple of God been neglected?"** Then I called all the Levites back again and restored them to their proper duties. And once more all the people of Judah began bringing their tithes of grain, new wine, and olive oil to the Temple storerooms."*

Nehemiah found other challenges upon his return to Jerusalem. In each case he confronted the problem with strong leadership. He describes his responses to the problematic issues, "So I confronted the leaders", "so I commanded", "I spoke sharply", "so I called down curses on them", "so I banished him", "I purged out everything" and finally, "I made sure". If one is looking for strong descriptions of leadership, look no further. If you are under the impression that good order can continue without constant care and attention from strong leaders, Nehemiah's story will explode that illusion. Life would be so much easier without the Second

Law at work. But the reality leaders face is that we are living in a fallen and cursed world -- one plagued with the Second Law of thermodynamics.

Immorality Enters the Church

Just because the examples cited are taken from the Old Testament do not get the wrong idea that things are somehow different today. This simply is not true; the same types of moral disorder and entropy that occurred in Old Testament Israel reappear in the New Testament Church as well.

The local church in the Greek city of Corinth is a prime example. The Corinthian church was one of the earliest congregations founded by the apostle Paul. It was located on an isthmus and seaport and the city became a large trading center in Greece. The apostle Paul visited this church personally, held it dear to his heart, and by his own admission, kept it in his prayers. Though his love was obvious for this group of believers, problems and scandals arose that compelled him to write them a stern letter to the church. He knew that if certain behaviors were tolerated and left unchecked they would have a very detrimental effect on the church.

He expresses his grave concern with these words:

*"**I can hardly believe the report** about the sexual immorality going on among you, something so evil that even the pagans don't do it. I am told that have a man in your church who is living in sin with his father's wife. And you are so proud of yourselves! Why aren't you mourning in sorrow and shame? And why haven't you removed this man from your fellowship?*

Even though I am not there with you in person, I am with you in the Spirit. Concerning the one who has done this, I have already passed judgment in the name of the Lord Jesus. You are to call a meeting of the church, and I will be there in spirit, and the power of the Lord Jesus will be with you as you meet. Then you must cast this man out of the church and into Satan's hands, so that his sinful nature will be destroyed and he himself will be saved when the Lord returns."

*How terrible that you should boast about your spirituality, and yet you let this sort of thing go on. **Don't you realize that if even one person is allowed to go on sinning, soon all will be affected?"***

Even though the church in Corinth had been founded by Paul, a man who had personal contact with Jesus himself, they still found themselves in the grip of the Second Law. If only church leaders today were ever aware of the possibility of entropy creeping into their congregation they could follow Paul's example and take strong pre-emptive action to nip it in the bud.

In this case Paul demonstrates the power of a leader who personally inserts the needed energy to challenge the onslaught of the Second Law. He directs that strong disciplinary action be taken by the leaders of the Corinthian church. Imposing discipline, whether in a church or business setting, is one form of opening the closed system and inserting the necessary energy and work to thwart the effects of entropy. Church discipline is a difficult and uncomfortable thing to do, which is why many leaders avoid practicing it altogether. This may be one of the biggest failings of today's church leaders. Why do church leaders hesitate to exercise discipline? Usually it stems from a variety of fears: the fear of confronting the offender, the fear of doing it wrong, or the fear of causing dissension among church members. Yet once spiritual entropy enters a church body, church discipline must be practiced if the church is to be kept healthy and strong.

> **Stop entropy at the earliest stage possible to suffer the fewest consequences possible.**

Paul explains one corollary truth of the Second Law, namely, that one bad apple does indeed spoil the bunch. Effective leaders know this and the Second Law demands this be the case. Therefore disorder is best dealt with in its budding stages, rather than addressing it after it has taken deep root. We all know that once a weed has grown deep roots, pulling it up can ruin the good plants as well. The lesson is clear: stop entropy at the earliest stage possible to suffer the fewest consequences possible.

One observation regarding church discipline is worth noting. t takes far less energy on the part of leaders to instill and maintain an acceptable level of discipline it is than to let things slide and then try and remedy the situation with a big bang. Small doses of energy that are consistently inserted into the system over the long haul are far better than one mega dose after the damage is done. It's the ounce of prevention thing that your grandmother may have mentioned to you. As one of my bosses at GM would remark, it's better to tighten the screws firmly at first then loosen them a little, than to come in later and have to really apply the torque.

> **Small doses of energy that are consistently inserted into the system over the long haul are far better than one mega does after the damage is done.**

The church where I served as an elder has a relatively minor, but somewhat aggravating, problem with discipline. As a group we were not particularly punctual. This in itself is not a big a deal, but when several worship services are conducted back to back, and youth activities must be concurrently coordinated, it can become problematic. As an example people often file into the main auditorium five and ten minutes after the singing starts. This is distracting to the people already singing at the beginning of the worship service. Yet, this problem has gone on for years and now we are a church that chronically runs about seven minutes behind schedule.

Our meager efforts at church discipline with regard to this habit, because they have been by and large meager, have proved unable to correct the problem. All our efforts have been met with passive aggressive behavior at best and active resistance at worst. Each "quick fix" has proved little more than a flash in the pan that quickly faded. Perhaps someday we will find the means to effectively overcome schedule entropy. This much I do know: if we are ever to succeed in this effort it will require a "big bang" of some sort. This form of entropy has gone unchecked for so long that it has become our culture. Fortunately, its impact is relatively small, but I wish we had shown decisive leadership to address the issue much earlier. But then again, I'm told I worry too much about the clock…

Energy from Leaders

It remains a mystery to me as to why God, who is all-powerful and self-sufficient, still chooses to accomplish his work through people. He must not be overly concerned about maximizing productivity or efficiency, because working through mortals is hardly a way to achieve either goal. Obviously, He must have oth-er goals in mind that are more important. There must be some other big payoff for him to have opted for this strategy. I suspect His true pleasure is in observing people growing into effective leaders. It must bring him immense satisfaction to watch peo-ple grow in wisdom, knowledge, and obedience as they lead the church. Otherwise, it might be very difficult for him to put up with all our shortcomings and mistakes. It helps to remember that much of what we are experiencing in life, even as we feebly grope our way along, is part of God's developmental process de-signed to prepare us for eternal life and service in heaven. It is something of a "trial and error here" for a "perfect service there" program.

So the burden to "open the system and infuse the energy" falls squarely upon the shoulders of leaders who must guard the health of the church. God promised the people of ancient Judah, "(I) *will give you leaders after my own heart, who will guide you with knowledge ad understanding.*" The leader's job is to be ever alert to the need for the infusion of new energy to keep the church in a healthy and growing state. **It will take a constant stream of energy for leaders to keep the church at a given level of health. It will take an exponential amount of energy to expand the kingdom and further impact the world for Christ.** King David summed up this principle extremely well as he prepared to pass the throne of Israel to his son Solomon, "*Be strong and courageous, and do the work. Don't be afraid or discouraged by the size of the task, for the LORD God, my God is with you. He will not fail you of forsake you.*"

The mantle of leadership is heavy. It is not to be placed on weak shoulders. Those who lead the church must be strong and courageous, and committed to continually "doing the work"!

Energy from the Spirit

So far our discussion has centered on the need for leaders to open the system, input new energy, and to do the work necessary to stave off the Second Law. The source of this new energy is one that the church must never overlook. It is the power that flows from God's Holy Spirit himself. In fact, all the other sources of energy pale horribly in comparison to the unending power found in God's Spirit.

God's Holy Spirit is the Third Person of the Trinity (or the Godhead as it sometimes referred to). The Scriptures teach that the Spirit is to be our guide, teacher, and comforter. He was given to us after Jesus ascended into heaven following his resurrection. Jesus remarked that the Holy Spirit would convict the world of sin, righteousness, and the judgment to come. Ultimately, he is the "power from on high" that enables the church to effectively carry out its mission in the world. Jesus also promised that Spirit would lead us "into all truth."

We are also taught that the Holy Spirit uses God's written word, the Bible, in a powerful way. In Hebrews we are told, *"For the word of God is full of **living power**. It is sharper than the sharpest knife, cutting deep into our innermost thoughts and desires. It exposes us for what we really are."* God's Holy Spirit uses the Bible in a way that injects energy and passion into individual lives and the church. As a result of the Spirit's active work the Bible is unlike any other book. It is alive! The Scriptures are full of life-giving power all on their own. Believers discover the Bible is one of God's primary ways to infuse fresh energy into our lives.

The Holy Spirit must never be overlooked when it comes to the energy needed to open the closed system of the church. God is after all, the only true source of energy in the universe. We need desperately to rely on him as our main source of energy in our battle against the tides of chaos and confusion. God has chosen to work through his people and his leaders. Yet they need to be vitally connected with God via his Spirit, His Word, and the constant communication of prayer.

The Head of the Church

The Bible teaches that Christ is the Head of the Church, and just as the head provides direction to the human body, so Christ provides direction to his spiritual body. Jesus is willing to invest all the energy necessary to both establish and keep his church. Ultimately, according to the Scriptures, the church will triumph even over the Second Law of Thermodynamics!

Allow a further explanation of this hope. We began the chapter with the observation that the Second Law was initiated as a result of the first sin of Adam and Eve. The introduction of the "curses" upon the earth opened the door to death -- the ultimate expression of the Second Law. Yet Jesus "opened the system" when he left heaven and took on the form of a man, being born of a virgin named Mary. He then "injected energy into the system" by living a perfect and sin free life. Finally, he provided the exponential energy required reversing the Second Law by allowing himself to be crucified and then rising from the dead. With this divine display of unlimited power, he was able to not only forestall the inevitable force of entropy, but to completely destroy it. **In heaven, the home of Christ, there is no second law of thermodynamics at work!**

When Christ returns to the earth the Second Law will be taken away with the same breath that created it. This much is certain -- the days are numbered of the reign of terror of the Second Law. Jesus has ensured its eventual demise. When Jesus cried out "It is finished!" as he hung upon the Cross, he cleared the way for the eventual "finish" of the Second Law as well.

The absence of the Second Law in heaven has a number of important implications. The Scriptures teach us that in heaven there will be no more tears. There will be no more sorrow or pain. Most importantly, there will be no more death, ever. The painful emotions and problems that bring tears, pain, sorrow, and death will be banished because the Second Law will be finally and forever rescinded. We will once again live the existence that we were created to live -- one without entropy, chaos and confusion.

This truth is captured vividly by John in Revelation when he wrote: *"Look, the home of God is now among his people! He will live with them, and they will be his people. God himself will be with them. He will remove all of their sorrows, and there will be no more death or sorrow or crying or pain. **For the old world and its evils are gone forever.**"*

*And the one sitting on the throne said, "Look, I am making all things new!" And then he said to me, "Write this down, for what I tell you is trustworthy and true." And he also said, **"It is finished!***

I am the Alpha and the Omega - the Beginning and the End. To all who are thirsty I will give the springs of the water of life without charge! All who are victorious will inherit all these blessings, and I will be their God, and they will be my children. But cowards who turn away from me, and unbelievers, and the corrupt, and murderers, and the immoral, and those who practice witchcraft, and idol worshipers, and all liars - their doom is in the lake that burns with fire and sulfur. This is the second death." **

This promised life in heaven, this blissful life unshackled from the curse of the Second Law of Thermodynamics, is freely available to all who will believe that Jesus Christ paid the penalty for Adam and Eve's first sin. Not only did he pay for that sin but all the sins we have committed since then. The new life Christ offers us is available to you if you are willing to believe he died in your place, you accept by faith his offer of salvation, and you put your complete trust in Christ alone for your salvation (rather than your own works or efforts).

It is a matter of simply trusting in the finished work of the Cross. When you make this choice to place your faith in Christ and what he has done that for you personally, heaven will be yours. The Bible tells us, *"For God so loved the world, that He gave his one and only Son, that whoever believes in him should not perish, but have everlasting life (John 3:16)."* You will begin to live the life that you were designed and engineered to live in the first place and ultimately end up in heaven.

The Mantle of Leadership

God has always chosen to work through people to lead his church. Being called to assume a leadership position in a local church is one of the greatest responsibilities in life that can be placed on a person. This is true regardless of the size of the leadership task -- whether serving as a nursery worker or Sunday school teacher or as a Pastor. As an Elder in my local church, the responsibilities I assumed were far greater than those that I carried as a senior executive with General Motors.

Though my leadership at GM impacted my company's ability to generate significant revenue streams, and though it affected the livelihood of countless people, it pales in comparison to the impact I could make as an elder in a local church. Why? My leadership at GM impacted the here and now, while my leadership at my church impacted people's lives for eternity. It's just that simple. Make no mistake, my responsibilities at GM were great and the burden seemed crushing at times. However, serving as an Elder of a local church is by far the most significant responsibility I will ever bear in this life because the stakes are so much higher.

Serving as a leader of Christ's church takes wisdom, courage, strength and unceasing love. To restate an earlier proposition: **The mantle of leadership is heavy, and it is not to be placed on weak shoulders**. As a leader you must be strong and have good courage, and you must do the work! This is what Paul meant when he penned, "*Therefore my dear brothers, stand firm. Let nothing move you. Always give yourselves fully to the work of the Lord, because you know that your labor in the Lord is not in vain.*" And one day the Second Law of Thermodynamics will surrender in defeat.

> **As a leader you must be strong and have good courage and you must do the work.**

BE STRONG AND OF GOOD COURAGE, DO THE WORK!

SECTION FOUR

CHAPTER 10

Pearls of Wisdom - The Leader
as a Mentor

"Do you mind if I ask you how your career got started?" The young engineer asked the probing question as we drove a prototype truck along a winding mountain road just northeast of Phoenix, Arizona. This was an important road test, and I was trying to concentrate on the ride character of the vehicle we hoped to bring to production in about three years. The engineer riding with me was responsible for "tuning" the springs and shock absorbers to give the pick-up truck the same ride as a luxury car.

After we had driven far enough to form my opinion of where I wanted him to take the tuning, it was time to answer his question. My response led to more probing questions on his part as, "How long should a person work at one assignment before they try to get a new one?" and "What kind of assignments should you pursue if your desire is to become a Chief Engineer?" Then he asked the tough one, "How do you manage your time wisely between your responsibilities at work and your wife and family?" A good question for a young man to ask being he was a newly-wed of just three months!

I am not sure why, but young engineers often ask me for similar advice. My administrative assistant understood how much I valued these opportunities to help people with their career decisions. She worked diligently to make room in my calendar to accommodate their request, and often squeezed the inquirers in during a lunch hour. They brought a brown bag lunch and we talked over a sandwich at my round table.

I make room because I believe that it is a leader's responsibility to coach and mentor others. If a leader has something of value to provide to an organization, they ought to value passing on their experiences and insights to subsequent leaders! Leaders should actively seek out ways to reproduce themselves in others.

Over the years I noticed a reoccurring pattern to the questions people would bring to the table. I've had ample opportunity to develop what I hope are good answers and advice (I never charge anyone for giving advice and thus can assure them they will get exactly what they have paid for.) In the next few pages I will illustrate some of the discussions that have occurred over the years. Hopefully these "Pearls of Wisdom" can be of assistance to those struggling with similar types of career questions or, help those leaders who, like me, are trying to develop future leaders.

A Successful Career

The morning after my conversation with the Ride Development Engineer, I had a similar discussion with a young female engineer as we flew out of Arizona. She had been working at our Desert Proving Ground in Mesa and I overheard her talking about a four-wheel drive development project. Being a truck Chief Engineer, my ears naturally perked up whenever I hear "four-wheel drive."

My daughter and I were seated in the same row with her for the 4-hour flight home. Jamie, my daughter who was home on winter break from Oakland University had accompanied me on this trip for some much needed sunshine, later expressed her amazement that before we were "wheels up" at the end of the runway I was drawing a diagram for this engineer. It was true; before we lifted off I started to explain how she could address questions she was facing regarding her next career assignment.

Her questions were similar to ones I encountered the day before, "What do I need to do to get an assignment as an Engineering Program Manager?" or "What jobs do I need to have to become a Vehicle Chief Engineer?" Some people are a bit more confused and want to know what they should be doing with their lives in general. In either case I begin by taking them back to the basics – what I look for when I seek candidates to fill positions I am directly responsible for.

My advice to the young woman on the flight, as it is to others, usually goes something like this:

"When I first became a manager and had to fill open staff positions, I primarily concentrated on the **skills** required to accomplish the job objectives. I looked at a position as simply a series of tasks to be completed --- tasks that required an individual working on them to be proficient in the necessary skills."

Then I draw a horizontal line on my white board (or scrap piece of paper if we happened to be sitting on a runway), and label it, "Skills."

SKILLS

I went on to explain, "I understood what skills were necessary for each job and so I set the standard for the particular skills required in order for people to qualify for the job." I then draw the vertical "Skills Required" indicator line.

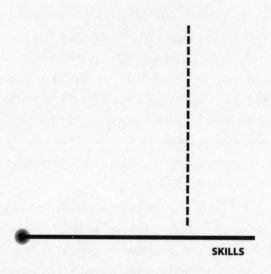

SKILLS

"However," I say, "I soon realized that this model was too simplistic. I did get qualified people to fill the open positions, but then later realized I often turned away applicants who were in the long run actually much better suited for the job." At this point I erase the requirements line and redraw it much lower on the scale.

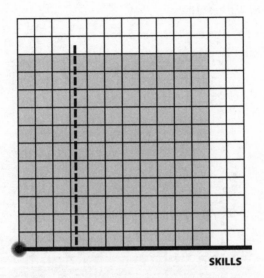

SKILLS

"As a result of loosening the skills required to apply standard, I was able to interview a much larger pool of candidates. This turned out to work OK for two reasons: First, I was able to select better candidates overall, and second, I realized that I could move people up the "Skills" chart without too much difficulty. All it takes is an investment of resources like time, coaching and training. Good people move up this scale pretty easily so this approach seemed to work out just fine." Now, often the people I'm coaching nod their understanding and agreement but it leaves them wondering "why is a less skilled individual a better potential hire?"

I explain it this way, "Moving this standard lower, yet finding better overall candidates, is an indication that there must be another dimension at play. There is, and I call it **Character**. Now the Human Resources department would like me to call this dimension 'Behavior'. Yet "Behavior" and "Character" are not truly synonyms. The real question is, "What kind of a person are we dealing with?" At this point I draw a vertical line on the diagram and label it "Character."

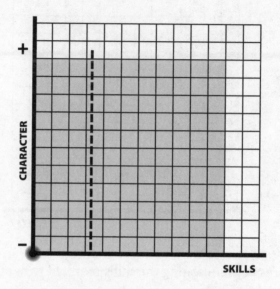

"Now unlike skills which you can measure and quantify for proficiency, you cannot measure character, so do not get too hung up on the scale. Suffice it to say, as far as character goes, you have saints and you have scoundrels." I indicate this continuum with a + sign and a – sign.

"Certain people are of unquestionable character and some are more dubious. Some people are very honest while others are disingenuous. Some people are industrious, ever willing to seek out new ways to be helpful and to put their shoulder to the wheel. Others develop a Teflon coated desk, where everything that comes to them just has a way of sliding right off. Nothing sticks!"

I often amplify the point with a personal illustration, "When my son was a young boy he began to develop a character trait I was quite concerned about. I would happen on his area of activity and immediately sense that something was amiss. (Fathers who were often in trouble themselves as a child have a nose for such things). I would ask, "Son, what is going on here?" It was at such times Justin demonstrated a unique ability to craft an answer that was as close to a positive response as possible, yet without actually lying!

After observing this on several occasions I sat him down for a father and son heart-to-heart talk. "Son," I began, "there is a difference between being honest and not lying. I do not want you to grow up to be a man that just does not lie. I want you to grow up to be an honest man! Simply not lying might be useful trait for a politician, but not for a man who carries on my name."

"Working in this business," I explain to young engineers, "where our product is concepts, ideas and intellectual property, honesty and truth are paramount. If I cannot trust a person they are useless to me. I would rather go with my own gut instinct and intuition than be misled with false data and bad information. I need blunt honesty. If it is an ugly baby, I need to know, it is an ugly baby!"

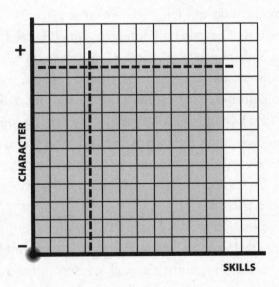

Usually, my listeners eagerly agree, and my co-passenger this morning was no exception.

I then draw another horizontal line indicating the "Acceptance" standard. It is placed very high, near the top of the chart.

"I place the bar in this dimension very high. I only want to surround myself and work with people of unquestioned character. I need to have complete trust and confidence in the people I work with."

I offer an illustration, "Often I will call one of my staff members to sit at my round table and commission them with a particular assignment. It is usually something on my "To Do List," and I delegate it to one of them. Now with my staff, as soon as they accept the assignment and leave my office, I delete the item from my list. I treat it as if the task has already been accomplished. They have not even traveled back to their own desk and yet I treat the assignment as if it were done. I know these people. I hired them. I trust them. I know their word is there bond, and they will move heaven and earth to accomplish what I have asked of them (and more if necessary!)."

"Now others do not fall into this same category. With those who have not yet earned my total trust once I give them the assignment and they get up to leave I will note on whatever document we were addressing, "f/u 2 weeks" (or some other appropriate time period). I then place this in my Out Box where my assistant files it in our "follow up file." Every morning she checks that file and places in my In-Box anything that was due to me on this date. Heaven help the ones who finds themselves popping up in my f/u in-box too often. I only want to work with those whom I can trust.

There is another reason I hold this bar high. Unlike the skills bar, which can be easily moved, this standard cannot be adjusted so easily. I simply cannot move character up for another person. Training a person to that high standard was their parent's job, and I cannot become a substitute for their unfinished work. Their parents had the responsibility to teach them to be honest, industrious, respectful, virtuous, courageous and moral. I cannot come in, after the fact, and input what their parents left out.

If time allows, I insert a parenthetical teaching moment into the conversation, "You should realize that this character bar can be moved. However, it is very hard to do so. To move a person up in this dimension requires the investment of a considerable amount of emotional capital. It is emotional capital I reserve for the training of my children, for investing in my wife, and in myself. What little remains I dedicate to polishing diamonds who are already above the bar and who could shine even brighter with encouragement.

With those investments in those close to me I'm spent. I do not have the additional emotional capital needed to invest in fixing people with severe character problems. I will inform them of their shortcomings and hold them accountable to demonstrate immediate corrective action. If they fail at that task, I simply work to free up that person's future and move them out of the company. Let them earn their bread somewhere else. There is no room for them here.

I often add an additional warning, "While it is difficult to move this bar upward, it does move in the downward direction quite easily. The Second Law of Thermodynamics insists that in a closed system, entropy must increase. As a result, unless one guards and works on their character continually, the bar will surely slip downward."

Take King David for instance. King David is spoken of in glowing terms in the Bible. He is referred to as "The apple of God's eye." Nowhere in Scripture is one man spoken of so fondly as David, from his youth on to his Kingship. David's stock became sky high and defined where the bar should be set for us all.

As you read the story of his life you are inspired by the greatness of his character and his impact on the world.

However, there came a point, even in this great man's life, when he let his guard down. A sad chapter in his biography begins with the words, "In the spring of the year, when kings go off to war, King David was on the roof of his palace." Why he was on a roof rather than with his men at battle is a legitimate question. From his perch he spotted a beautiful woman named Bathsheba taking a bath. David wanted her, and as a result he had an adulterous affair with her.

In that instant his stock plummeted and from that point onward his life story becomes sad and troubled. Take this as a warning. You must guard your character diligently. Every morning when I shave (I look the protégée in the eye) I tell myself, "Greater men than you have failed. Guard your heart!' You should do the same.

I then draw an oval in the upper right hand corner and explain, "Wherever you are on this chart, you always want to be moving in this direction." I draw an arrow to the upper right hand quadrant.

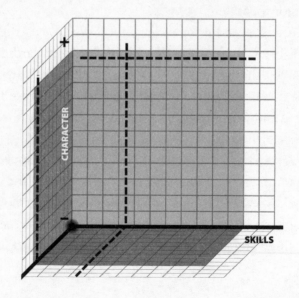

"Whatever your next job, make your aim at that assignment to grow your skills. Seek out a job that you do not know how to do, something that will put you a little off balance and even make you uncomfortable. You want to be learning and growing always! You want your toolbox filled with new tools. Some people look into their toolbox and all they have is a hammer. Now a hammer is a fine tool, but if it is your only tool, you will be forced to look at every problem as if it were a nail. Not a bad approach if the problem is a nail, but if it is a bolt than needs a wrench, a hammer is a poor tool to attack it with. If your problem is with a person, using a hammer is even worse! Get my point?" They always do and usually with a smile.

> **Constantly work on yourself as a person. Ask yourself what are you doing to guard your character?**

"Constantly work on yourself as a person. Ask yourself what are you doing to guard your character? What biographies and autobiographies are you reading to learn from the successes and failures of other great men and women? What energy are you pouring into yourself as a person, to be healthy in mind, body and spirit? These things are important and you must never neglect them."

Sometimes I illustrate with a brief recounting of the life of President Abraham Lincoln. Along the skills axis, I explain that although he was born with precious little as far as worldly wealth, Lincoln moved up the skills axis his entire life.

He taught himself to read. He learned the mathematics and enough trigonometry to become a surveyor at a time when our county was growing and people were staking out boundaries. He taught himself enough law to become an attorney so he could help people settle boundary disputes created by poor surveying. He taught himself to become a judge, an orator, an assemblyman, and a statesman. He even taught himself to become a President!

"As far as character goes, history has very little to say relative to his flaws. This is not because the biographers choose to be kind. On the contrary, they usually relish an opportunity to expose flaws and dirt in the life of any person of note. There just seems to be very little anyone can find to write bad about him. In fact, Stephen Douglas, his opponent for the Senate, is quoted as saying, "Abraham Lincoln is the most honest man I know." Now how is that for a scathing rebuke? How would you like even your enemies to say that about you?"

Lincoln is often cited as having said, "I will study and prepare, and perhaps someday my chance will come." He simply moved in the direction of this arrow all his life, taking control of whatever he had control over. "And perhaps someday my chance will come," indicates that he left the uncontrollable to Providence. And his chance did come. And he was killed for it, but that's another story."

When it appears all this is starting to sink in, I add a few bricks to the load with this comment, "As I worked on this mental model of career success, I began to realize that this model is still too simplistic – there is yet another dimension at work. I have noticed something very special about certain people who become the best of the best." I draw another diagram off to the side that looks like a typical bell shaped curve.

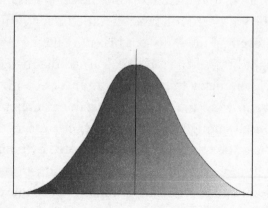

"There are some people who are really not very good at their craft at all and the company would be a better place if they were not employed here. We all know these types of people." I point to the lower left hand tail of the curve.

"Then there are the multitudes of individuals that define "average," the ordinary, the expected or the norm." I point to the very center and uppermost portion of the curve.

"But then there are those who are special, those who define the very best at what they do. They are the best of the best." I point to the tail at the right of the curve. "What is it about these people that make them the very best?"

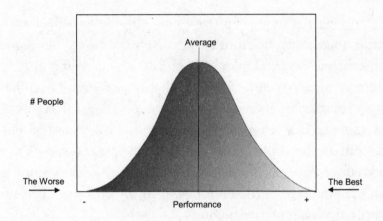

After kicking around a few ideas I draw yet a third dimension on the original skills/character chart. It makes it a little cluttered, but if the protégé have stuck with me, it works. I break the tension when I label the third axis, **"Talent"**.

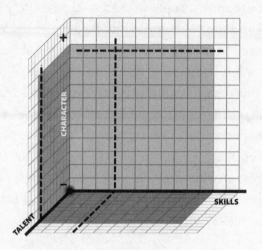

This is where things get interesting. "All people are born with certain unique talents. From birth, you are hardwired in unique and amazing ways. Think about it: from the dawning of time until now there has never been another one of you. I find that simply amazing." I go on to explain that our DNA can combine in a vast number of ways. "Some scientists calculate that our DNA can combine in at least $1 \times 10^{2,400,000,000}$ power. That is a one with 2, 400,000,000 zeros behind it. That's a larger number than the predicted particles of matter in the universe. It is no surprise that each of us is unique."

"In fact, God spoke to one of his prophets, one named Jeremiah, and He told him, "Jeremiah, before I formed you in the womb, I knew you." He could say the same thing about each of us because we are all uniquely formed. We were hard wired in a special way from birth. The question is, "What makes you unique? What is special about you?"

"One way to explore your uniqueness is to examine how you are talented. As you were developing as a baby certain aspects of the neural network of your brain were forming super highways of data flow, while other pathways were atrophying to near uselessness. The result is that in certain areas of life you are very capable, while in others, you are probably rather inept."

"Let me give you another personal example. When my son was a young boy, I had hoped he would someday become an engineer, just like me. I don't think that is so unusual, a man wanting his son to follow in his footsteps. Yet as he completed middle school and then high school it became painfully evident that he did not seem to have an analytical molecule in his body. He couldn't take the derivative of X^2 if his life depended on it (for those interested the answer is $2X$). The left side of his brain seems to idle at about room temperature. However, as time passed, I was increasingly awed and amazed at the creative talents that he possessed. He can take a hunk of clay and carve and chip away at it until it looks more like a gorilla's head that you can find in the zoo.

"Today when you put a movie camera in his hands, along with a good editing program, you will be thrilled as he makes the world come alive right before your eyes! He is incredibly talented and on his way to becoming a great movie director."

"Now if you give me a hunk of clay and ask me to sculpt a gorilla's head, I will need some drafting tools, a full scale model to work from, a sterolithography computer-controlled prototyping tool, and then maybe, just maybe, it will turn out looking like an animal. Justin is talented at the arts, and I am analytical."

"The key is this: you need to find the areas that you have talent in and then work there to exploit your talents to the fullest. You need to find the design space where your talents lay and move in that direction with your career. This is the combination that the Best of the Best seem to possess!"

"For example, I know a woman who has a very special and obvious talent. Her name is Laura and her talent is "compassion." Now, I am not totally devoid of compassion, but let's just say that it neither consumes nor drives me. Imagine that I am standing in a crowd, say following a church service. A bunch of kids are tearing around the lobby letting loose all the energy they held in check in Sunday School. Perhaps one of them falls and scrapes his knee and he begins to cry.

"Now if he is within reasonable walking distance of me, say, no more than three steps, I may go over to him and help him up. At that point I have just two concerns: are you bleeding and how can I get you to stop crying? This may be a character flaw on my part, but I hope you see the point I'm trying to make."

"I will usually say something to the hurting child like this, 'Here, let me see that knee. Wow, that's cool, you got a good scrape. Does it hurt when I push on it like this?' I'll push on or near the wound. This usually accomplishes the desired effect. I get to see that no stitches are required and it really startles them!"

'Yow!' they yell. Some will actually laugh at the absurdity of the situation. How could anyone do something so strange as to make a boo-boo hurt even more? Others just look at me with the question, "Who are you and why in the world are you pretending to make this hurt even more?" Either way, I get them to stop their mental cycle of feeling hurt and sorry for themselves. They soon stop crying, quickly gather themselves and go on their way, running once again."

I'm not sure exactly what they are thinking as they take off, but by my actions I tried to say, "Hey there, Son, get tough. It's a rough world out here. Suck it up and pull yourself togeth-er. Come on now, be a man. After all, big boys don't cry over scraped knees.' I know -- you don't have to tell me -- I'm a bad person -- at least one who lacks the talent of compassion."

"Now I have witnessed Laura encounter the same situation many times. If Laura is aware that someone has fallen she will immediately move toward them regardless of how inconvenient the location or timing. She will not stand the child up but rather bend down and ask them if she can 'see it'. She then says, 'Oh boy, you got quite a scrape there. I bet that really hurts, doesn't it?" She invites the tears, and they run naturally into her hands as she gently touches the little face. 'How about if we go in and put some Neosporin on it and cover it with a Band-Aid?' She lifts them up and guides them toward restored health."

"I am pretty sure that when they leave her care they are indeed feeling better. More importantly they are feeling loved and cared for. As they take off running again, they know that if they get hurt there is someone who will love them and take care of them. I am glad there are people like Laura in this world."

"Now guess what Laura does for a living?" Without waiting long I gladly share the answer, "She is a nurse. Can you imagine that? A person who is gifted and talented at compassion makes her living as a nurse! As nurses go, she is the best of the best on the floor."

"My wife delivered our third child via a difficult Cesarean section at the hospital where Laura works. It was amazing to watch Shelly's countenance change when Laura entered the room. She brightened up and was immediately encouraged by her presence. She actually started to heal faster. It was an amazing to watch the impact of her talent on others."

I point back to the diagram and the Skills axis in particular, "Shelly had a lot of nurses. I am quite sure that they all had the necessary skills to do their jobs well. They understood sterile fields, pharmacology, IV administration and countless other skills of the trade. I did not see any of them drop their thermometers on the floor and then pick them up and put them in her mouth. They were all skilled."

I then point to the Character axis, "And as far as I could see, they all seemed to be people of good character. They all came to their shifts on time, did not look hung over, and as far as I could tell, were not stealing drugs out of the narcotics cabinet."

"But this one, the talent dimension, is now the discriminator. Many people become nurses for various reasons. Yet, not many become nurses because they are talented at compassion. These people do not want to feel the pain that the patient is feeling. They do not want to feel the loss if the patient dies or even if they get well and leave when they are discharged. They do not want to bring home the pain and suffering, some of which they have had to create in the process of healing others. As a result they build a callus around their hearts. They build an invisible wall around their own vulnerability and they learn to care for others from a distance."

"Not Laura. She enters the patients' pain. She allows herself to be open and vulnerable to the hurt of others and tries desperately to help ease it. She accepts the fact she will experience pain if she loses a patient that she has become close to. It is her talent, it is in her nature, and she resonates when she practices it. When one operates at resonance they get out substantially more than they put in! That is what makes her the best nurse on the floor."

Turning back to the diagram I continue, "You need to understand where your talents reside and then move in the direction were you can exploit them to the fullest. You need to find the design space where you will resonate, and put your full efforts into that space.

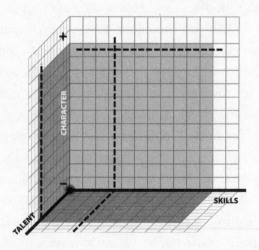

"So as we look forward to where you would like to go with your career," I continue, trying to help them make sense of my three dimensional drawing, "you need to make sure that you are constantly learning, and growing your skill base. You want a full tool box which enables you to take on higher and higher responsibilities."

"You need to be a person of unquestioned character, one who is used as a role model for others to emulate. You want to constantly work on who you are as a person, in body, mind and spirit. You are not a human doing, you are a human being. You want to be a person who continually guards their character."

> **You need to be a person of unquestioned character, one who is used as a role model for others to emulate.**

"Then you want to move your career in ways that can exploit your natural talents." At this point I draw the desired target area for the individual. "It is really a lot more complicated than I can illustrate here, because a person has many talents, not just one. But you get the picture."

"For instance, one of my talents is talking. Now as shameful as that may seem, it is actually a very useful talent for a leader. There are times when I need to talk with journalist as we launch a new product. I speak with groups of engineers at design reviews and town hall meetings to give direction and hopefully encouragement. I speak with lawyers, executives and legislators. I give interviews for trade magazines and I speak before students at major universities. The ability to speak is a talent that I can exploit in my assignment. Each job has that opportunity."

This is often a good place to end the generic discussion and segue into more specifics issues. Sometimes, however, I am asked how one finds their own unique talents. This is a little tricky, because I believe I am getting close to trying to do the job parents should be doing. A parent needs to train up their child in the way they are naturally bent and hard-wired. But if it is too late for that to happen, then I advise an exploration period. Trial and error is a good scientific method and it can work here too. This is why college intern programs are so beneficial. A person can try on several areas of the business to see how they each "fit". They may leave a temporary assignment and say, "I will never do that kind of work again!" That is fine. They learned something and they can go on from there.

Conversely, they can experience areas that they feel excellent about. They get good feedback and hear phrases like, "Well done," or "Hey, that was great." When you get input like that you are on to something. Look for where you resonate, where you seem to get more out of a situation than what you feed into it. Look for times when the day flies by and you look forward to coming in the next day to take up where you left off. These are good signs.

I usually end this part of the conversation with these words, "This is just a mental model that I have been using to help guide career decisions. It is a work in process and is not yet complete. But I hope it helps. It is very hard to describe what a successful career is. That is a deep and complex subject. But I do know what it is not. It has nothing to do with the level or position that you eventually end up at. It has nothing to do with the house you live in or the clothes you wear. Which axis here describes what kind of a watch you sport on your wrist? None of them do. Which axis asks how much money you have? Again -- none of them. I know many very wealthy people,

> **You will find success when you grow your skills, live your life of integrity and virtue, and learn to employ your talents.**

and to be honest with you, most I would not trade places with for two minutes."

"I believe that you will find success when you grow your skills, live a life of integrity and virtue, and learn to employ your talents. If you are fortunate enough to do that in an area where you can dedicate yourself to something significant, something bigger or someone greater than yourself, at the end of the day you will be fortunate enough to say, 'I have been successful.'"

Read, Study and Hang

At GM, I often took a few minutes a week to walk up and down the corridors of our engineering building with one of my staff, or with others that I was mentoring. Our building seemed to be about a half mile long, and walking the long halls gave us a few minutes to break away from the tyranny of the urgent. They provided us those few precious moments just to talk.

When our discussions focus on leadership, I advise my protégées to read. Leaders need to read. I suggest that they read all the biographies and autobiographies that they can find time to study. I advise that they pick out different types of leaders from all walks of life. Leaders from the arenas of the military, politics, business, religion, sports and academia are all good individuals to study. What made these leaders tick? How did they get their start? What motivated them? What made them the best? How did they handle success, and more importantly, how did they handle the failures they encountered along the way?

Fortunately there are also shelves full of books written on the topic of leadership, this volume included. It is a huge topic and it is helpful to look at it from a wide variety of perspectives. If you're bent towards the technical and scientific, hopefully this book will speak to you from that unique perspective.

Reading is fundamental to leadership development. One thing I do is list all the books I read, including those in my library at home and the office, and I would post these on my web page at General Motors. This way I communicate "The Chief's Recommended Reading" material.

Someone once asked me how a person can become wise. It was one of the best questions that I have ever been asked. I could not offer a cookbook answer, yet I did share that if they truly want to be wise they should hang out with other wise people. I believe this is true. If you hang out with dopes, chances are, you will become dopey yourself. If you spend time with wise people you will likely catch how they think and act. The opportunity is then yours to adopt some of their habits for you own.

The same advice is true for leadership. If you want to become a great leader try hanging out with great leaders. You can do that both by reading about them, or, better yet, by spending real time with them.

> **If you want to become a great leader try hanging out with great leaders.**

One method is to ask an effective leader to become your mentor. I usually have about six to twelve active protégées that I mentor on a regular basis, and countless others who just stop in just for a chat. This proves a good opportunity for both of us to sharpen our leadership skills.

Another way to increase your leadership aptitude is to volunteer to take on leadership responsibilities. When I was a young engineer, I realized that my supervisor often talked about difficulties with his budget. I recognized that I did not have a clue as to how to manage a budget, but that if I aspired to take his job someday, and I surely did, then I would need to learn to do so. So I asked him if I could manage the budget for the department and he gladly let me. He taught me how to do it and he stayed close since he was ultimately responsible, but that gave us great opportunities to sit and talk. These discussions almost always transcended the budget. We ended up talking about personnel issues, business strategy, and office politics. I learned more from his personal tutoring than I did in any other single assignment.

The world is hungry for effective leaders. The community you live in likely needs people to stand up and assume leadership roles. The local school boards, townships, churches and charity organizations are all hungry for people to take on the mantle of leadership. If you wish to practice the art of leadership I can assure you there are ample opportunities available right now, the Zeroth Law ensures this is true. Just as a medical doctor practices medicine, leaders should practice leading others.

Teach, Coach and Mentor

There is an old saying that goes like this, "If you really want to understand something, teach it." That thought definitely holds for leadership. If you want to hone your skills in leadership you will sharpen them when you try to teach others about the subject.

One thing that happens whenever we attempt to teach or coach others about leadership is that it gives one the opportunity to explore what they really know and believe with respect to the topic. You perhaps have had opportunities to lead, some of which were very successful, and if you are like me, some of which were miserable failures. So what did you learn from your successes? What really worked well? And what did you learn from your failures? I don't think any of us should overlook those. In life we seem to learn much more from our failed attempts than we do from our successes.

As you try to communicate your thoughts to others it forces you to first sort them out for yourself. You will find yourself highly motivated to do this well, knowing others are depending on you to offer them sage advice.

This careful preparation becomes paramount whenever you accept the opportunity to speak on the subject of leadership.

There are ample opportunities within technical, social and academic circles to share your ideas on the importance and style of leadership you hold dear. Public speaking is an excellent proving ground to test and focus your own ideals regarding leadership.

On a more personal level, you should look for opportunities to mentor those who will need to develop their own leadership. Again, leaders must reproduce themselves in others and pass on whatever insight and knowledge they can to capable hands that will follow them. If each generation were to stand on the shoulders of the giants of the previous generation, what a tall people we would become.

Therefore, a leader has the responsibility to teach, coach and mentor those you come in contact with who demonstrate that spark of inspiration and motivation characteristic of nascent leaders. Leadership is not of the masses, and it never will be. The Zeroth law prevents it. When the special ones rise above to take on the responsibility of leadership, to become the higher source of energy, it is the established leader's responsibility to guide and teach them.

A caution: ***The mantle of leadership is heavy. It is not to be placed on weak shoulders.*** Established leaders must place the mantle only on the strong shoulders and then commit to continuing to strengthen and encourage those who bravely take the burden on themselves.

Accountability and Follow-Up

One talent that a leader needs to possess by nature, and if they do not, a skill they must learn, is the ability to make complicated things simple. This applies both to incoming information as well as outgoing communications and directives.

With regard to incoming information I have found two elements that require constant attention. The first, for lack of a better or more discrete term, I call the "BS Filter." I wish I could count how many times people have brought forward presentations overselling a position, or worse, full of fluff and eye candy. They are designed to cover up the fact that very little useful information is currently available.

When I determine that a person is speaking about something they do not know much about, or extrapolating well beyond what is reasonable given the information they are privy to, then I call an immediate halt. I have been told that my left eyebrow rises perceptibly in proportion to the amount of "bs" I am being exposed to. Good managers in my division have come to recognize this ominous warning sign and quickly withdraw the speaker from the floor. They are sent immediately back to the drawing board to get their facts straight. It is rumored that my eyebrow signal has saved many a young career from an early demise!

The second element I give conscious attention to is the tendency for others to try and place their monkey on my back. This happens most commonly with people who see themselves as "victims" of unfavorable circumstances or processes. They do not feel that it is fair that their lives be disrupted and inconvenienced by things beyond their control.

As one folk proverb sums it up, "Too bad, so sad." Bad things do happen to good people all the time, and the monkey they end up with on their back is indeed theirs, whether it deserves to be or not. Leaders need to be aware that some people who find themselves in such a situation are indeed uncomfortable, but leaders can ill afford to take on each person's difficulties for themselves. Instead, leaders should try to understand the person's situation and insure that proper resources are being employed to rectify the situation in a timely fashion.

This same "bs filter" employed above needs to be applied to outgoing messages too. People need and want to hear the truth, with simplicity and accuracy. The Scriptures promise that the truth will set you free, and indeed it will. The sooner we acknowledge the truth of a situation, the sooner everyone can adapt to the facts and take the appropriate actions. Time and again people have commented on how much they appreciate my direct, albeit blunt approach to communications. I have even been told that I am "gifted in bluntness." The pay-off lies in the fact that nobody wastes time trying to figure out what they were just told. I try to be clear and direct. It may not always be pleasant news, but it is intended to be understandable and actionable.

I try and take this same direct approach with my emotions. I do not make a very good poker player for the simple reason I have a hard time bluffing. I wear my emotions on my sleeve and what you see is what you get. After one difficult meeting an engineer came up to me and asked if I was upset with what had transpired. "If you have to ask, I am not. If I am, you will know," was my response. People want to know where they stand and a good leader lets them know that clearly.

With simplicity, must also be consistency of behavior. My entire organization knows that I insist on a few block and tackle type elements fundamental to our work. Of the hundreds of metrics that could be applied to determine how well we run our business, I hold four of them dear: (1) I insist that we get our engineering released on time; (2) That we build and ship our test properties on time; (3) That we resolve our design issues on time, and (4) That we validate our designs on time.

The engineers have heard me state these basic tenants hundreds of times, and often repeat them themselves. I base merit raises on their performance based on these objectives and reward those who consistently accomplish them with high quality. They have become affectionately known as "The Big Four," and everyone who I have worked with in the past who puts their effort into engineering one of GM's Full Size Trucks knows them by heart. The constant insistence of achieving these objectives has resulted in a culture that delivers all four on a regular basis.

A leader needs to be consistent in regard to insisting on such fundamentals so they become predictable and understood by those charged with delivering on them. It is then that individuals within the organization can make clear decisions on their own to accomplish these fundamentals, understanding they are of paramount importance to the organization.

The accepted behavior standards of the organization should also be communicated consistently and with simplicity. The leader needs to establish the high standard and then consistently live up to that same standard themselves. People come to work to succeed, and the leader should recognize that fact. Leaders must expect and insist on the best from their people and themselves if they hope to accomplish great things.

I witnessed the simple statement of the standard held dear by the Plant Manager at the time at GM's Pontiac East Assembly Plant where I worked for two years. I was responsible for the operations of the Paint Shop and Body Shop at the plant. One of the standards held dear was that we would insist on a clean and safe working environment. One day early in my tour of duty I was walking through the plant with the Plant Manager. As we walked down an aisle we happened upon a piece of paper, a part identification tag of some sort, which had fallen off one of the thousands of vehicles being assembled at that moment. The Plant Manager automatically stooped down, picked it up, and crumpled it in his hand. He later dropped it in a trash can further down the way.

The standard was clear: he expected a clean shop and he picked up any piece of debris that he came across. You do not have to witness that happen too many times to get the picture: it is your responsibility to keep your work area spotless and free of debris. From then on I never hesitated to stop and pick up any debris or trash that dared mar the appearance of one of my shops. I soon noticed my superintendents doing the same.

Leaders must constantly be aware that they lead by their actions much more effectively than they do with their words. Your actions speak so loudly hardly any-one can hear what you are saying!

> **Leaders must constantly be aware that they lead by their actions much more effectively than they do with their words.**

Recognition and Reward

There is a fact that is true of each person I come into contact with: they all want to feel signifi-cant. Life is too short, hard and difficult for it to have no ultimate meaning. Each of us wants to be part of something bigger than ourselves, to be part of something lasting, to be part of some-thing of significant.

This is why one of the worst punishments in our prison sys-tem is to strip a person of their personal identity and then assign them absolutely meaningless work. This robs a person of their basic need to belong, and to be counted for something.

This human drive for significance is fundamental and deep and needs to be addressed by the leader. As a leader you need to develop a strong focus and awareness of the people's need to be recognized and rewarded for their efforts and outstanding work. Of all the skills that a leader needs to develop giving appropriate recognition may be one of the most important. People are willing to suffer through grueling ordeals on the trail of tears to success; they will consider it the most significant period of their career if their labor and achievement is duly recognized and rewarded.

Early on in my career as the Assistant Chief Engineer of Full Size Truck Development, we uncovered a problem with one of the engine accessories that was going to be used in all of our truck products. This problem would adversely impact every truck model we were going to produce, so the ramifications of the situation were immense. We had arrived at a stop order condition with the entire fleet at risk.

It became my responsibility to lead a cadre of engineers from all across the corporation in understanding and resolving the problem. The work pace was intense and continued virtually around the clock. The pressure was on to deliver and I felt that pressure resting squarely on my shoulders. Though in reality it fell on many shoulders, I had given my word to management's upper echelon that the problem would be fixed in time to start our normal production.

As it turned out we resolved the problem. We accomplished the equivalent of about two years of engineering in two months time. What is interesting is that to this day I consider those notably awful 60 days as among the best of my entire career. I still have a model of the compressor we redesigned mounted on a plaque in my office as a vivid reminder of what we accomplished. My wife will attest that these were among the hardest two months of my career; yet with the favorable outcome, the recognition and reward that followed, I can honestly say it was one of the best periods I can remember.

As a leader you need to realize that words of encouragement and recognition of the skill, talent and labor of those you lead is not only a nicety, it is a necessity. Recognition is the lubricant required to keep the efforts of your team moving against the friction that the second law demands to impede them. Recognition is the injection of energy needed to overcome that natural loss, and to propel the charges on to success. Done well, done sincerely, recognition is a force multiplier.

During my staff meeting we focus some of our time on stand out, valiant acts and the appropriate ways of recognizing them are discussed. Forms of recognition vary as much as acts of valor do, but let me offer a few examples of effective recognition that does not require a great expenditure of budget.

A Card

One effective form of recognition is writing a personal note in your own handwriting. I keep a stack of personalized cards, that I use to send a quick note of thanks or wish someone well. I also take advantage of e-mail cards which allow me to type a note. While these electronic methods work fine, there is still nothing more compelling than writing a card using ink from your own pen to convey your heart's thoughts. Though my penmanship at times resembles Egyptian hieroglyphs, the investment of my time and effort seems to communicate far more than the actual words.

If I hear that someone is suffering from a health problem, or one of their loved ones is, or something noteworthy comes to my attention, I quickly jot a note to send a card later on. I challenge you to make this exercise one of the top five things you intend to accomplish each day. Then watch and see if your investment in the hearts of those you lead is not richly rewarded.

A Coffee Mug, With Coffee

When I was a Chief Engineer of Full Size Trucks, we purchased a few cases of coffee mugs from our petty cash account. They were black with white lettering with our logo and the words, "Full Size Truck Engineering." On the opposite side are the words, "Take No Prisoners," printed in a jagged font. The latter is our motto that says at FST we will do whatever it takes to be successful.

There was a "Take No Prisoners" event when I was scheduled to meet two of our engineers. My prior appointment was running late and taking away from their promised time. My Administrative Assistant knew the nature of my first appointment and directed them to the location where I was tied up. It created a bit of a stir when they found me lying supine on a cot giving a pint of blood at the Red Cross area set up in our building. I had nothing better to do, so we discussed business while I "gave the last full measure." Their presentation, however, elevated my blood pressure and I think I may have set a record in filling the donor bag. (All done, of course, in the Take No Prisoners spirit!)

When someone does perform above and beyond the call of duty, we would present them with FST TNP coffee mug. We may have arrange for the recipient to come to my office for a private presentation. Other times we may have invited the person into a staff meeting and present them with the mug as we detail for everyone that person's heroic actions.

This method has proved a very inexpensive, but highly effective means, to communicate our gratitude from exceptional behavior. FST Take No Prisoners coffee mugs are considered a badge of honor and people aspire to earn one.

One other note: After several years I discovered the best part of the presentation occurs when we stop everything and go to the coffee station for the inaugural free "fill-up" on me. Never underestimate the value of personal face-to-face time. It is what employees remember most.

A Public Display

I attend numerous events that demonstrated that our product is engineered to the desired state and we can now move on to the next stage of the production process. Getting to this point is often required incredibly long hours and the best efforts of many individuals. It is one thing to declare that the team has been successful, success was always the goal. It is another thing to offer specific and appropriate words of acknowledgment and recognition in a public forum. This recognition seems to hold the longest lasting value for the people honored. Years after an event, people will casually share with me that comments I made that continue to motivate them to excellence today.

As Proverb tells us, *"A word aptly spoken is like apples of gold in settings of silver."* If a leader could develop one skill and hone it to a fine edge it would be the skill of speaking words of recognition and gratitude from their heart. This is another powerful force multiplier!

A Visit

Another effective tool is to drop in on a team meeting that normally you don't attend and offer words of praise and recognition. Going to someone else's turf to acknowledge them in a personal way sends a powerful message.

It is also important to pay a personal visit in times of crisis in people's lives. If humanly possible, I always attend the visitation or funeral of one of our employees or of their loved ones. This expression of personal concern is almost mandatory for an effective leader.

This truth hit me hard when my father passed away. I was a young executive when Harold Woychowski, my dad, passed away. Many of his friends, relatives and co-workers at GM came to pay their respects along with several of my own close friends. I was moved to tears, however, when during the wake I noticed one of our Executive Vice Presidents, Guy Briggs, walking into the funeral home to pay his respects.

While my own supervisors did not visit that night, this great man had traveled a long distance from his home on his own valuable time – all to honor my father and show compassion to me. He will never know how much that meant to me. From that day onward he owned my undying loyalty. There is nothing within the bounds of morality that he could ask that I would not do for him.

I also try to visit employees who are in the hospital. Setting aside a few minutes to see them and offer support is simply the right thing to do as a leader. It is impossible to overestimate the importance of personal visits in times like these.

A Weekend Away

While it's unnecessary to have a big budget for effective recognition, at times it can help. We occasionally will provide a weekend away for an employee and their family as a form of thanks. This is usually reserved for the individual who consistently has sacrificed their own time (and that of their family's) in the service of the company. While a spouse and children are not on the direct payroll, they often make large sacrifices along with the one who is. Rewarding them with a weekend away is a tangible way to remind them that they are truly invaluable to our success.

A VME

Voice Mail can be a helpful technology and is proving quite useful as a recognition tool. I will leave a quick message in a person's VME box when time does not allow for a card and an immediate word is more valuable. I will typically leave a VME message on an associate's birthdays or another special occasion.

I use voice mail in another special way. When the children of one of my staff do something noteworthy enough to deserve bragging rights at our daily staff briefing, I will send that child a voice mail message. This ranges from achieving an "A" on a math test to earning a Varsity Letter. I smile as I imagine Mom or Dad sitting on the phone at home catching up on the latest VME traffic, then calling a child over to the phone and saying, "Hey, this one is for you!" If you want to be a blessing to someone special, bless their children.

A Merit Raise

Perhaps the most formal of all recognition awards is the merit raise. Too often in the past, corporations viewed it as the inevitable outcome of simply showing up for work each day. I tailor my merit fund to benefit those whose character, talents and skills constantly produce great results. To do otherwise is to reward incorrect behavior at the expense of the opportunity to reward excellent behavior. Entropy will always seek to dominate the merit world, so as leaders we need to exercise the energy to direct merit raises in the right direction.

Relationships

One common thread ties together all these different forms of recognition: relationships. These acts of recognition either result from building strong relationships or they are forming the foundation of new ones.

You will never know to send a VME to a deserving child unless you first have the relationship with a parent that allows them to tell you about the special achievement. Nor can you provide meaningful recognition to others unless you sincerely mean it, and to do so, you must build a relationship.

In a complex organization, especially one that is organized in a matrixed fashion, nothing is as important as the relationship between the employee and their direct supervisor. Nothing! That being the case, it is the leader's responsibility to focus on building strong relationships and demonstrate their importance by your actions.

One vital aspect of this is meeting people where they are. The Apostle Paul said that he *"became all things to all people that he might win some."* Jesus always met people where they were. He was as at ease speaking with a prostitute as he was conversing with a king or governor. Likewise, an effective leader should be as comfortable chatting with a member of the Board of Directors as they are talking to an hourly employee installing axles in an Assembly Plant. The ability to do this may come from a variety of sources: a sense of self-confidence, a willingness to meet new people and learn about their lives, or a genuine desire to show respect to everyone you meet.

It may be a skill difficult for some to develop but it is well worth the effort.

Leading by Serving

As I draw to a close, I have saved the most important concept in effective leadership for the last. It is the one idea that ought to shape and define our mental model or paradigm of leadership.

Simply stated it is this: The leader is a servant.

> **The leader is the servant.**

When I began to work my way upward to increasing levels of leadership within the ranks of GM, I started with the wrong idea of leadership. I thought if I could only become a leader then things would get much easier for me. I would not have to worry as much about the success of my projects. After all, it seemed that all my supervisors had to do was demand perfection from me and then it was my job to deliver on it. I reasoned that if I could be the boss, then I wouldn't have to constantly compete to be the best. I could just sit back and enjoy the scenery. I would let everybody else bust their backsides to accomplish the impossible.

Oh, what foolish thoughts run through the minds of youth! (Or as someone else has put it, youth is wasted on the young.)

As it so often turns out in life truth is just the opposite of what you think. The burden of success ultimately rests on the shoulders of the leader. In fact, if done right, leadership becomes a thankless endeavor. Much like a professional sports coach, if the team does win a championship the credit will go to the players who are expert athletes, who worked together unselfishly and in harmony. You will go unnoticed.

But if they fail, then it is obviously the coach's fault for not leading effectively, and he or she has got to go. So it is with all true leadership. It may appear the leader is the one being served. Ultimately, however, directions are given for the good of those executing the mission, and every difficulty met along the way must be ultimately seen as the responsibility of the leader, not the players.

For the leader to ultimately succeed they must view themselves as the servant to those they have been charged to lead. The leader must be constantly searching for new ways to assist the team to succeed in the mission that has been assigned. They must insure that their people have the necessary resources required to complete their tasks. They must also insure that the mission itself is logical and legitimate. They must staff their ranks with talented people of unquestionable character. They must train them intentionally to complete their tasks. They must constantly be on the look out for areas of trouble and confusion, giving direction and making decisions to steer them clear of the dangers. Like shepherds, they must constantly be on the look out for trouble lurking in the shadows, and be prepared to swiftly address the foe when it attacks.

One of Colin Powell's leadership maxims is that you want your people to feel free to bring their problems to your attention. He believes that when people stop bringing you their problems, you have stopped being their leader.

Our desire is typically to have everything go along as smoothly as possible. This side of heaven that notion is living in a fool's paradise. The Laws of Thermodynamics will not allow it -- it is the leader's job to address difficulties. Do not grow tired of doing this; it is your duty.

Jesus said that He did not come here to be served, but to serve. If that was His attitude, how much more should we adopt it for ourselves?

Summary

So there we have it.

The Three Laws of Thermodynamics lend themselves to the understanding of the Three Laws of Leadership. As with all of nature, these laws are irrefutable and are no respecter of persons. The sooner we understand them, even own them, the better prepared we are to fulfill the Bible's Great Commission to subdue and have dominion over the earth.

The Zeroth Law of Leadership insists the masses cannot lead themselves and that a leader must rise to do so. If the leader is not you, then who? If it is not now, then when? Think about that when you consider your own leadership.

The First Law of Leadership says you cannot create resources out of thin air and that therefore you must seek the greater good in every decision you make. Do you demand that people accomplish something great, given nothing? Or do you recognize that every decision is a commitment of precious resources that must be directed to the greatest good?

Remember, anyone can choose between good and bad. Do you have the wisdom to discern what the greater good is and focus your resources to that end? Do you have the fortitude and courage to walk away form good things in the journey to accomplish great things? If you do not, who will? If you do not do it now, when will you?

The Second Law states that everything will tend in the direction of disorder, chaos and confusion – all of its own accord. You do not have to wait for the competition to come along and decimate your organization; nature is willing to do it for them. A leader must understand it is up to you to constantly inject the needed energy into the system to confront and reverse this destroying force. Are you constantly putting your personal presence and commitment, your passion and your power, into your areas of responsibility? Are you ever aware of the fact that left alone, disaster awaits you at the door? If you do not, who will? If you don't respond to it now, when will you?

Remember that **the mantle of leadership is heavy**. It is not to be placed on weak shoulders. If it has been placed on yours, may God bless you and strengthen you.

Be strong and of good courage, and do the work!

About the Author

Terry J. Woychowski obtained his dream job in 1998 when he was appointed the Vehicle Chief Engineer for the General Motors Full Size Truck Platform. The Chevrolet, GMC, Cadillac and Hummer trucks he helped create where highly successful in the market, won numerous industry awards and generated multiple billions of dollars of profit for the company. It was in these intense and challenging environments and other assignments like this that he forged his own leadership skills, and ingrained his commitment to help develop leadership skills into those he worked with.

Terry's ubiquitous engineering talents were developed in his home environment where his father, Harold J. Woychowski, growing up in a rural farming community in the thumb of Michigan enlisted his sons to assist in the repair and maintenance of every family owned car, truck and appliance that required attention. After moving to the suburbs of Detroit his father became a Technician at the General Motors Noise and Vibration Laboratory. At dinner he often spoke of tough engineering problems to be solved and the many challenging assignments he faced. When Terry announced that he too wanted to become a Technician at the Noise and Vibration Lab at the GM Milford Proving Ground, his father said no. He was encouraged instead to attend college, to obtain a degree in Engineering, and then to get hired by GM and to become his father's boss. With this vision Terry attended Michigan Technological University and in four years' time earned his BS in Mechanical Engineering. Directly out of college he was hired by General Motors and became a Test Engineer at the NVL, where for a brief period he became his father's boss. Terry completed his career at GM after 33 years, where he had become the Global Vice President of Program Management, and then as the Global Vice President of Quality and Vehicle Launch.

Terry retained his affinity for Michigan Technological University where he was invited to serve on the College of Engineering Advisory Board. In 2007 he was honored by being inducted into the Michigan Technological University Academy of Mechanical Engineering and Engineering Mechanics. The Academy honors distinguished alumni for excellence and leadership in engineering and civic affairs. Later, Michigan Governor Rick Snyder appointed Terry to serve on the Michigan Technological University Board of Control, where he is the Chairman of the Academic Affairs Committee and serves of the Leadership Committee and the Michigan Tech Fund. Terry was awarded his Doctorate in Business Management, honorus causa, from Indiana Wesleyan University in December of 2003.

Terry has devoted much time to the support and furtherance of the engineering profession and STEM (science, technology, engineering and math) education. Terry has served on the Board of Directors of the Engineering Society of Detroit where he served as the President Elect, the Chair of the Young Engineers Council and then as its President for two years. During his time at the ESD he orchestrated a trilateral partnership with the ESD, MTU and GM to create and offer a retraining program for displaced engineers in the southeast Michigan area who wished to retool themselves and prepare for job opportunities in the growing area of advanced propulsion. This effort has been repeated several times and has developed into a Master's Degree program at MTU. Terry is a member of the Executive Leadership Team of Project Lead the Way, a STEM based educational program designed to introduce the engineering disciplines into elementary, middle school and high school programs. He is often requested to provide key note addresses in STEM education and community service forums.

Terry remains involved in many civic outreaches as well. He has traveled to Port-au-Prince Hattie to assist in relief efforts following their devastating earthquakes as well as to Albania to assist in the establishment of refugee camps for victims fleeing from the Kosovo conflict in the Balkans. He founded the Woychowski Charitable Corporation (foundation) and enlisted his children and their spouses as the board of directors. Together they have sponsored several Michigan Tech Senior Design project teams to design and build human powered grain mills. Partnering with World Hope International, several of these mills have been built and deployed in villages in Zambia Africa.

After retiring from GM, Terry was appointed as the Senior Vice President of Engineering and Quality at the American Axle & Manufacturing (AAM) company. He resides in Commerce Michigan with his wife Rochelle.

terrywoychowski.com